The Administrator's Guide
to Whole Language

The Administrator's Guide to Whole Language

Gail Heald-Taylor

RICHARD C. OWEN PUBLISHERS, INC., Katonah, New York

RICHARD C. OWEN PUBLISHERS, INC.
135 Katonah Avenue
Katonah, New York 10536

PRINTED IN THE UNITED STATES OF AMERICA

Book design by Ken Venezio

Dedication

I dedicate this book to my Mom
who taught me perserverance.

Contents

Preface   ix

1. Foundations   3

    Building a Personal Foundation   3
    Background in Whole Language   3
    Whole Language Philosophy   4
    Comparison of Approaches   7
    Principles of Whole Language   15

2. Whole Language Strategies   19

3. Common Questions about Whole Language   37

4. Implementation   51

    The Principal's Role in Implementing Whole Language   51
    School-Based Implementation   53
    Assessing a Whole Language School   60
    Assessing Principal's Effectiveness in Implementing
        Whole Language   78

5. Making the Transition from Traditional Approaches to
    Whole Language   83

    Appendix   Checklist for Whole Language Basals   89

6. Informing Parents about Whole Language   93

   Building Parent Support for Whole Language   93
   Whole Language Tips for Parents   105

7. Assessing Student Growth   109

   Student Evaluation   109
   Reporting to Parents and Whole Language Report Cards   127

8. Whole Language Research: Key Studies and
   Reference Literature   149

   Resource Materials for Whole Language   149

   Bibliography   175

   Index   187

Preface

The overwhelming interest in the whole language movement, shared with me by principals and superintendents, has prompted the writing of this book. Administrators tell me that you are reading about whole language in journals, are hearing about it at conferences, are observing your teachers implementing it in your schools, and are being encouraged by local language arts consultants to support its use schoolwide. Some of you are intrigued by whole language; others are very interested; and many of you have become converted. You want to become actively involved and are asking how you can support the growth of whole language in the school. You wonder what resources you should purchase; how you can respond to philosophical questions teachers and parents ask regarding the use of basal readers, phonics, and spelling; and how you can encourage teachers to implement whole language in their classrooms.

Administrators' interest in whole language is especially important now because research proves that successful implementation of any new curriculum is dependent upon the support of principals. Indeed, the role of the principal is cited as one of the key factors in determining the success or failure of an innovation. It is not surprising, then, that positive implementation of whole language is greatly facilitated by your understanding, involvement, and leadership.

Most whole language in-service and professional reading materials are directed to classroom teachers. Although these resources are also very useful for you, they do not necessarily address those issues that are important for administrators.

Principals play a unique role in the whole language movement. Their questions and requirements are different from those of teachers. For example, the key focus for the principal is the school; whereas for teachers it is the classroom. Principals are interested in the basic differences between approaches in language instruction so that more informed decisions about the purchase of materials for the school can be made. But teachers want to know the philosophy of language approaches so that they can choose appropriate instructional materials for their particular grade levels. Principals are interested in identifying the various whole language strategies in order to promote their use by teachers in the school. Teachers want to know how to use whole language strategies with groups of students. Evaluation is a concern of principals so that progress in the school can be identified for superintendents and parents. Teachers are more concerned with individual language growth. Principals want to implement whole language across a school. Teachers want to implement whole language at the grade level.

Principals also play a unique role with parents. While parents want to hear from their children's teachers how language arts is taught, their questions and concerns usually are communicated through the principal. It is in the area of schoolwide implementation that principals will make the greatest contribution to the success of whole language.

To date, whole language implementation has been anything but systematic. Its growth has largely depended on individual teachers who have been exposed to a single workshop, a conference, or a guest speaker, and then return to their classrooms expecting to implement whole language often without practical resources or the support of colleagues, principals, or consultants. Some teachers develop networks with other teachers so as to nurture their budding interest. But for a few, the obstacles are simply too great and whole language withers and dies. But now, with the emerging interest of principals in the whole language movement, combined with current research in school-based implementation procedures for schools, the potential for successful implementation of whole language is greatly enhanced.

This book is for those of you who are interested in learning more about whole language. It is not intended to persuade those who doubt or feel skeptical about whole language. Much has already been written for those who are not persuaded. Instead, the book is designed for those of you who already have an awareness of and support for whole language philosophy and are looking for information and answers to some of your related questions. This is a "how to" book: It provides an explanation of whole language philosophy that can be shared with teachers and parents;

it responds to key questions asked about whole language by teachers and parents; it identifies the key whole language strategies; it provides a whole language school-based implementation process for you to use in leading the staff toward successful whole language implementation; it shares ways to assess a whole language school; it shares strategies for gaining parental support for whole language; it provides alternative evaluation strategies for your teachers to use in evaluating whole language; it gives samples of whole language report cards; it provides a thumbnail sketch of current research studies that support whole language philosophy; and it presents practical resources and classroom materials for your teachers.

—G. H.-T.

The Administrator's Guide
to Whole Language

1. Foundations

BUILDING A PERSONAL FOUNDATION

It may be difficult for you not to start implementing whole language at once, but rushing into implementation before laying appropriate groundwork can ultimately be counterproductive. For example, generating staff excitement and interest for a whole language initiative before gaining philosophical and financial commitment from superintendents could result in the lowering of staff morale when there are no funds for conferences or out-of-school visits. Thrusting your whole language goal onto a staff without involving them in the decision automatically breeds their resistance. One principal with whom I worked couldn't understand why after a year of whole language implementation only one of a staff of ten had begun to use whole language strategies. When I talked to staff members in the principal's absence they complained that whole language was hers, not theirs. Although they were somewhat interested in it, their principal couldn't explain to them what whole language was, couldn't identify whole language strategies they should use, nor answer any of their questions about it. No wonder they were disenchanted. Therefore, developing a background in whole language yourself is vital.

BACKGROUND IN WHOLE LANGUAGE

While it is not imperative that the principal be an expert in whole language philosophy in order to lead successful implementation in the school, having a basic understanding and some ready resources at hand to share with teachers and parents can be a great asset to you.

Principals implementing whole language report that they are frequently asked by teachers and parents about its origins, how whole language is different from skills-based approaches, what the principles of whole language are, and what instructional strategies are used. I have prepared some background information related to these areas that you may use with your teachers and parents when you begin to implement whole language. Each topic is written so that it may be used as a mini-resource article for teachers or parents at a future in-service session.

WHOLE LANGUAGE PHILOSOPHY

Whole language philosophy is not new. At the turn of the century educator John Dewey advocated student-centered, activity-based learning (Dewey, 1902, 1929). Psychologist Jean Piaget also contributed theories of developmental learning from 1940 until the 1970s. For generations educators have valued the use of holistic strategies (that is, strategies concerned with all the systems of learning) such as literature of quality for reading instruction and the use of the child's recorded oral language to build the foundations of writing and reading (Roach Van Allen, 1982; Stauffer, 1970). For the past fifty years language arts programs have used some elements of holistic learning. Such elements include the incorporation of language experience (printed records of children's oral language), or times when teachers read quality literature selections to their students and encouraged them to read books from the school library; when they encouraged dramatic presentations and role plays related to stories in literature; and when they set up activity centers where students could interpret some of the literature that had been read to them. But until the 1980s language programs had an eclectic composition with a heavy emphasis on skill activities, controlled language readers, and a liberal dose of phonetic instruction. Holistic strategies were often only considered when time permitted.

As research in the 1970s and 1980s was conducted, a gradual paradigm shift occurred away from eclectic language arts programs in favor of an holistic view. Five areas of research supported this shift:

1. developmental learning
2. oral language development
3. reading

4. writing
5. evaluation

Developmental learning was supported by Carol Chomsky's research in oral language (1969) and Elizabeth Sulzby and William Teale's work with emergent reading and writing (1983–1987). Their research clearly demonstrated that pre-school children learn language developmentally, rather than through formal instruction, when they experience literate-rich environments where they engage in talking, reading, and writing experiences.

Research in oral language development from 1960 to 1985 provided the foundation for whole language philosophy. Carol Chomsky's research in oral language showed that pre-schoolers learned to speak as they engaged in talk with significant others around them. It also showed that children develop their own rule systems as their oral language emerges. John Aitchison's research in Great Britain in 1973 and Dan Slobin's work in 1985 confirmed that children acquire language naturally rather than through formal instruction.

These findings had a profound effect on researchers of reading who surmised that if oral language was acquired and not taught then what about learning to read? Research by Dolores Durkin (1965), Don Holdaway (1967–1979), and David Doake (1977–1980) of pre-school readers showed that pre-schoolers who read before coming to school did so without formal instruction in letter recognition, phonetics, or word drill. Marie Clay's work (1967) demonstrated that mature readers don't use phonetic cueing systems and that an overreliance on phonics actually retards reading progress. Frank Smith's findings in 1969 demonstrated that isolated vocabulary study interfered with comprehension. Jean Lutz's study (1974) criticized American basal texts for their short, simple, monotonous, and sterile sentences. Clay's research and Russell Stauffer's (1960–1965) indicated that children learned to read better when texts retained the natural qualities of the child's oral language. Doake (1980) and Holdaway (1979) advocated a read together process using quality literature selections. The implications of this research prompted a movement away from direct instruction of letters, phonetics, and words (the approach so commonly used in basals) and supported the use of literature-based, comprehension-focused strategies for reading instruction.

Research on children's writing in the 1970s and 1980s supported the principles reported in oral language and reading research: that writing was learned developmentally rather than through direct teaching. Clay (1972–1974) and Diane De Ford (1977–1978) indicated that pre-schoolers were able to communicate messages through drawings and scribble even before they were concerned with conventional letters. Heald-Taylor's work (1981–1983) showed that some first-grade children record stories through scribble and random letters. Chomsky's research (1968–1969), Charles Read's work (1967–1975), and Richard Gentry's study (1980) documented children's use of invented spellings (spelling approximations) from pre-phonemic (no evidence of sound-symbol relationships) to standard spellings. It was Donald Graves' work (1972–1986) and that of his colleagues, Lucy McCormick Calkins and Susan Sowers, that provided a wealth of data documenting the writing process (drafting, conferencing, revising, redrafting, editing, and publishing). They showed that children's writing starts with an initial draft. Students are encouraged to share their first drafts with adults or peers who hold conferences with them (talk about the draft) by sharing the parts they like, by asking about missing information, or questioning aspects they don't understand. Writers are invited to respond to these conferences by making changes to the compositions. Several conference and revision sessions may take place, depending on the number of changes the authors want to make. When authors are satisfied with their stories, they edit for spelling, grammar, and usage before the stories are published.

This research in writing has profound implications for classroom practice because it is critical of former classroom writing practices that focused on skill instruction in grammar and spelling at the expense of composition. Instead, research supports a student-focused writing program that includes daily writing, developmental spelling, conferencing and revising, and the fostering of skills in the context of the writing itself.

Research in evaluation supports a shift away from standardized tests of skills toward evaluation by observation. David Pearson and his colleagues (1985) and William Teale and his colleagues (1987) are critical of standardized tests because they are based on outdated language research. Standardized tests are simplistic and ignore emergent reading and writing behaviors. Formal tests have a questionable aura of objectivity. This research suggests that observing students while they are engaged in reading or writing provides a more reliable source of valid information about students' growth in language.

This research in developmental learning, oral language, reading, writing, and evaluation is called whole language when it is applied to classroom practice.

COMPARISON OF APPROACHES

One of the most common questions principals ask is: "What is the difference between whole language and a skills-based approach?" It is a difficult question to answer because whole language is a belief system, a way of understanding learning, a view of instructional processes; and that is difficult to put into words, especially if one is expected to compare it with a skills-based approach. There is probably no real program in existence that exemplifies a pure skills-based or pure whole language approach that a writer could use as a practical means for comparison. Most teachers employ a lot of strategies from both approaches in the hope of presenting some sort of balance and at the same time reflecting each teacher's philosophical beliefs about how children learn. When attempting to compare the two approaches writers may simplistically apply a "black hat" label to skills-based strategies and a "white hat" label to whole language, ignoring the fact that traditional strategies used for generations did in fact produce youngsters who could read and write.

Despite difficulties in comparing a skills-based approach to a whole language approach, it can be a worthwhile exercise in order to gain an appreciation for the obvious differences as well as the similarities.

Both approaches have the same basic goal, the desire that youngsters learn to read and write well. They are also both concerned with skills; that is, the need for phonics, word recognition, grammar knowledge, spelling ability, an appreciation for literature, and skill in developing coherent compositions. The key differences between the approaches are in the philosophy of how children learn, the teaching strategies used, the materials used for instruction, the role of the teacher, and evaluation methods. We must remind ourselves as well that both approaches work. Generations of youngsters have learned to read and write using skills-based approaches, but we also know that youngsters are becoming readers and writers using whole language strategies. In reality, most youngsters have probably become literate through the use of both philosophies.

For comparison purposes I am going to take a polarized view by dealing with each approach in its idealistically pure form, even though no real program is absolutely skills-based nor completely whole language based. I have chosen to discuss the area of reading and then writing instruction separately despite my belief that they should be integrated in a quality language arts program. The result may be somewhat artificial but also useful for understanding the basic differences between the two approaches.

Reading

Philosophy   The philosophy of skills-based reading programs is centered on learning theories of the behavioral psychologists of the 1930s and 1940s. These psychologists supported the principle that students learn simple concepts first and complex concepts later through the introduction and drill of a sequentially organized hierarchy of sub-skills. Reading was thought to be a composite of sub-skills such as letter recognition, sound-symbol association, and word knowledge. It was believed that if teachers formally taught each sub-skill and drilled the children in it until mastery was obtained before moving on to the next set of sub-skills, students would eventually learn to read. Great emphasis was placed on learning the sequential parts so that understanding of reading eventually could take place.

The philosophy of whole language programs is based on developmental research of the 1970s and 1980s in the areas of oral language, reading, and writing in which children are actually engaged. Researchers agree that language learning is a highly complex process that children can deal with right from birth. For example, this research indicates that children master the complexities of oral language before the age of five, and many have begun to read and write by that time as well. Such children are not formally taught, nor have they sequentially mastered the sub-skills of talking (sounds of phonetics, vocabulary, grammar skills) before they are communicating in sentences and in holding conversations.

In whole language it is believed that reading and writing can be learned in the same natural way as children learn oral language. To support reading growth youngsters are introduced to entire stories first, rather than sub-skills, and are encouraged to understand the meaning of the stories before they are expected to master the reading of individual words. Whole language programs are meaning driven rather than skills driven, and the instructional materials, teaching methodology, and learning activities are consequently planned to encourage understanding of literature.

Instructional Materials In skills-based programs reading materials are usually designed and written by educational psychologists and reading experts. The texts are usually contrived to accommodate the phonetic skill previously taught or the word lesson. Therefore texts usually emphasize sound-symbol relationships within individual words and the repetition of pre-taught vocabulary. For example, some stories use only words with the vowel "a" because the other vowels have not yet been taught. A page of text may look like this:

Dan has a ham. A ham, a ham.
Look Sam, Dan has a ham.

Skill learning and mastery is the goal, not the meaning of the text. In skills-based programs teachers are expected to instruct youngsters formally in letter recognition, phonetics, sight vocabulary, and grammar, and then to reinforce the mastery of these sub-skills through letter-name exercises, phonetic workbooks, or fill-in-the-blank grammar and comprehension sheets. "Sounding out" is the key reading strategy emphasized when students read unfamiliar texts.

In whole language programs reading material that has been written by authors of children's literature is used. Selections are chosen based on their literary merit and their ability to capture the interest and imagination of youngsters. Students are introduced to complex language syntax, varieties of genre, descriptive language, and different story structures right from the start. Since initially meaning of text is considered more important than mastery of sub-skills, children are exposed to and encouraged to appreciate numerous selections before they are expected to read stories word for word. Although teachers introduce new literature selections daily, they ̣o rehearse many of the old favorites each day. Children are encouraged to learn to read as they are guided in the reading process, learning the various reading skills as they actively participate in reading literature selections. This is different from the skills-based approach where they would master a series of sub-skills before they actually begin to read stories. In whole language classrooms teachers lead the children toward independent reading by modeling the reading of good literature for them, by engaging youngsters in the reading process, and by gradually introducing students to varieties of reading skills. Initially the teacher reads the selection to the children and then re-reads a portion to them, expecting the children to "chime in" as they recognize the pattern, refrain, or rhyme.

Youngsters are constantly encouraged to use a variety of strategies as they begin to read independently. These include picture clues, memory, retelling, word pointing, noting the pattern of the sentence, concepts of the story, and meaning of the text, as well as phonetics. Gradually each begins to read word for word in both familiar and unfamiliar texts.

Students usually engage in follow-up activities such as illustrating a page of rehearsed text, listening to familiar stories at the listening center, dramatizing stories at the puppet theater, painting scenes from favorite stories, or writing their own compositions. In whole language programs listening, speaking, reading, and writing activities are integrated because they interrelate and support the reading process.

Evaluation   In skills-based programs teachers evaluate student progress by children's knowledge of phonetics, recognition of sight words, ability to complete worksheets, oral reading of basal level texts, and performance on standardized tests.

In whole language programs teachers note each youngster's level of understanding of literature, observe the varieties of strategies each uses in independent reading (meaning, picture clues, pattern of story, word pointing, and phonetics), and check each child's appreciation for the varieties of literary genre and authors. Language behavior inventories and checklists are more widely used than standardized tests.

Writing

Writing strategies in skills-based programs are not grounded in any real research. Rather, it has always been assumed that writing strategies, like reading strategies, should be based on the prerequisite learning of writing sub-skills. It is presumed that when the sub-skills of handwriting, phonics, spelling, grammar, and usage are pre-taught, composition writing will automatically benefit. Because the sub-skills are thought to be so important, instructional time for skills far outweigh that devoted to the composing process. When students do write, the topics and genre are usually chosen by the teacher, probably based on a particular skill the teacher wishes to reinforce.

Writing instruction in the whole language approach is based on a considerable amount of research conducted during the 1970s and 1980s. This research indicates that skill in writing develops more dramatically when youngsters spend most of their time engaged in the process of communicating ideas rather than the overemphasis on the pre-teaching of writing sub-skills. In whole language clarity of communication is the primary focus of writing instruction, and skills in handwriting, phonetics, spelling, grammar, and usage develop within the act of writing or in individual and small group interviews. In whole language children, rather than teachers, choose the topics and genre about which to write, and they are encouraged to write about things they know a lot about. Youngsters are given opportunities to communicate stories even before they have mastered the sub-skills of writing, and are therefore allowed to dictate stories, draw pictures, use scribble or invented letters, as well as incomplete (invented) spellings to record their stories. Thus, children are invited to write on the first day of school, rather than waiting until the end of first grade or beginning of second grade when children have mastered some of the sub-skills of handwriting, phonics, and spelling, and have begun to read, as is practiced in skills-based writing programs.

The key difference between skills-based writing programs and writing instruction in whole language classrooms is in the writing process itself. In skills-based writing classrooms the writing process consists of:

1. a skills lesson
2. teachers assign the writing genre and writing topic
3. students write a draft of the composition
4. students correct spelling, grammar, and usage errors
5. students write the final draft

In whole language classrooms students experience the writing process as real authors do:

1. students choose topics about which to write
2. they write a draft
3. students share their drafts with peers or the teacher
4. students confer with teacher or peers to determine if the piece is clear, needs more information, or would benefit from more detail
5. students often redraft and confer several times before they are satisfied with the piece

6. although editing occurs at all phases of the writing process, as they read and redraft their pieces, students also formally edit their work before preparing final copy
7. final copy is often typed by a teacher or volunteer.

Skill development is important to both approaches, but is dealt with quite differently in each. In a skills-based approach the learning of adjectives, for example, is introduced in a formal lesson, and then students are required to write a descriptive paragraph in which they are encouraged to incorporate numerous adjectives. In a whole language classroom the way real authors describe settings, characters, and action is modeled through the literature students are reading. The teacher invites students to share their use of descriptive language in their own writing efforts, and then students are encouraged to build more descriptive detail into their future compositions.

Knowledge of skills of spelling, grammar, and usage are also dealt with differently in each approach. In a skills-based approach these skills are formally taught and reinforced through skill exercises in spelling, grammar, and usage. In whole language classrooms teachers share with children the skills they already practice in their writing efforts, and then, according to the needs of the class, give small-group instruction on particular skills. Teachers also give individuals advice on skill development during one-on-one conferences, as well as on the running anecdotal record kept in each student's writing folder.

Another key difference in the two approaches is in the area of evaluation. In skills-based writing programs compositions are primarily evaluated according to proficiency in skill areas, rather than for composing strategies. For example, skills of spelling, grammar, and usage are usually evaluated with more weighting than the clarity of the written product; and the writing process is rarely evaluated at all.

In whole language classrooms teachers monitor the strategies students use in the writing process itself: the student's ability to share drafts, listen to responses to the writing, and make changes in the writing so it is clear to the audience. Teachers in whole language classrooms also note the writing strategies students use in their final compositions, such as the use of exciting lead sentences; the description of settings, characters, and action; the use of detail; the varieties of ways to end a story; and the use of different genre, including narrative, realistic fiction, fact, mystery, letters, poetry, research, etc. Students are also evaluated for their developing skills in spelling, grammar, and usage, and the editing strategies they use. A skills-based language program and a whole language approach are similar yet different in many ways as has been shown: in philosophy, instructional methods, learning process, and evaluation. Table 1.1 highlights the key differences.

Table 1.1
Comparison of Skills-Based and Whole Language Methods

Reading Method Used by Teacher	
Skills-Based	*Whole Language*
teaches segments from part to whole in a hierarchical order	models the reading process from whole to part
letters	reads whole stories (literature,
sound symbols	dictated stories)
words	invites child to get involved in the
phrases	reading process
sentences	invites child to:
drills words	reconstruct a whole story through
uses controlled readers	retelling or rereading
teaches skills in isolation	discuss the meaning of the text
	predict events
	apply concepts in the story to his/ her own experiences
	read and reread familiar stories
	read independently

Learning Process by Child	
Skills-Based	*Whole Language*
learns letter names	seeks to understand the whole text
learns sound-symbol relationships	learns from whole to part
learns isolated words	reconstructs the whole story in a
reads controlled vocabulary in phrases	literature selection or dictated story
reads controlled sentences	understands the meaning of the text
reads stories with simplified text	matches story to a specific page
	develops directionality and tracking (word points)
	uses picture clues
	identifies repeated sentences and phrases
	identifies familiar words
	develops phonetic awareness

Reading Material	
Skills-Based	*Whole Language*
controlled vocabulary texts basal phonic booklets	predictable texts literature, dictated stories, sentence strips, pattern books, student published material trade books, novels, factual books

Evaluation	
Skills-Based	*Whole Language*

phonetic knowledge
word knowledge
worksheets
skills tests
basal level
standardized tests
	observation of language behavior as children are engaged in reading and writing
	reading
	  use of meaning
	  use of pictures
	  use of patterns
	  use of tracking (pointing)
	  use of phonetics
	  comprehension through class discussion
	reading behavior inventories

Writing Method Used by Teacher	
Skills-Based	*Whole Language*
emphasizes skills *before* composing teaches skills of spelling teaches grammar in isolation teaches punctuation and usage separately controls topics and genre controls format of writing expects transfer of learning to students' compositions	promotes daily writing encourages experimentation (allows invented marks and spellings) encourages drafting and revising emphasizes composition development encourages growth of spelling, grammar, usage *within* process of writing links literature to writing encourages development of composition through conference interviews and drafting encourages students to publish writing recognizes developmental stages

Learning Process by Child	
Skills-Based	*Whole Language*
learns spelling lists	gets "hooked" on writing
learns phonic rules	enjoys writing
learns punctuation	drafts and revises
learns grammar rules	learns conventional spelling, grammar, usage within process of writing
	attends to grammar, spelling in revising, editing, and publishing processes

Writing Experiences	
Skills-Based	*Whole Language*
teacher assigned	*daily* writing opportunities
skill-oriented exercises	student-selected topics
teacher-controlled topics	student choice of genre
teacher-controlled genre	revising encouraged
weekly writing opportunities	draft writing encouraged
	publication of student efforts emphasized

Evaluation	
Skills-Based	*Whole Language*
emphasizes knowledge of isolated skills	emphasizes integrated growth of composition and conventions as students write
spelling tests	observation of growth in:
grammar tests	composition
usage tests	symbolic representation
composition evaluation based on deficits of spelling, grammar, usage	spelling
	conventions
	publishing, revising, editing
	writing behavior inventories of actual behavior of students in writing process

PRINCIPLES OF WHOLE LANGUAGE

Whole language is governed by some important principles that are quite different from skills-based approaches. In whole language it is believed that youngsters acquire language rather than learn through direct teaching; that language learning is child-centered, not teacher-dominated; that language is integrated rather than fragmented; that children learn by talking and doing rather than through passive listening; that they learn to read and write by engaging in experiences with literature and writing, as opposed to drills and workbook exercises; and that children learn best in interactive problem-solving situations rather than in isolated individual tasks. The key principles of whole language follow.

Acquisition of Language   Language is acquired in a complex, interactive, social process as youngsters engage in listening and reading complete stories; tell and write comprehensive tales; and interpret their feelings and thoughts through other language events such as drama, creative arts, music, movement, discussion, writing, and investigation.

Child-Centered   Whole language strategies build on the vast warehouse of knowledge children bring with them from home, are designed for both student and teacher initiation, encourage active involvement by students and teachers, meet the needs and interests of individual children while allowing each to progress at his or her own rate.

Integration   In whole language classrooms students experience the complex language process as they engage in real language events that integrate and interrelate listening, speaking, reading, writing, visual arts, and drama, as well as other content areas in the curriculum (science, social studies, mathematics, music, etc.).

Oral Language   Whole language classrooms foster talk to facilitate thinking and writing when youngsters dictate personal stories and as they co-operatively learn through discussions in the various activity centers in the classroom (puppets, art, drama, construction, sand, water, book, viewing, etc.).

Literature   Quality, stimulating, high-impact, unabridged literature is the basis for whole language learning that youngsters will hear read to them; that they will be encouraged to read for themselves; and that will stimulate them to be involved in creative writing, drama, and art.

Writing In whole language classrooms students write every day for a variety of purposes about topics they choose; and are allowed, in the initial stages, to represent their stories through drawings, dictation, retellings, and invented marks (scribble) or letters. Through individual conferences students are encouraged to respond to their own stories and the writing of others, to revise through drafts, to edit, and to publish their written compositions.

Problem-Solving Learners in whole language classrooms continually predict, hypothesize, test out, generalize, and confirm their developing language in speaking, reading, and writing; their language grows steadily, and sometimes dramatically, from approximation to standard form.

Groupings Students are involved in a variety of groupings—whole class, small group, and individual learning situations.

Self-Concept In whole language classrooms students feel they are effective, competent, capable, and knowledgeable language users.

2. Whole Language Strategies

Principals often ask for a definition of a whole language strategy. Such a challenge invites at best a simplistic response to a very complex notion, and yet I believe the question is valid. The characteristics of a whole language strategy, in my view, is a language situation that is student-focused, process-oriented, and links many language processes (listening, speaking, reading, writing, drama, interpretation through the arts, thinking, and problem-solving).

The personal dictated story is a good example of a whole language strategy. It is student-oriented because it emerges from individual students rather than from the teacher, since the story topic comes from the child's real-life experiences or from literature the youngster has heard or read. The story itself is controlled by the student author as he or she decides how to start, which information to include, how detailed the events will be, and when to end the composition. Through personal dictation many language processes are integrated (thinking, oral language, composing, reading, listening, writing, and the arts). For example, developing a story to tell involves both thinking and composing, while oral language (speaking) is the vehicle the student uses to share the story. When the teacher writes the story down the conventions of print and writing are modeled as the student sees the use of standard letters, spaces between words, complete spellings, capitals, and punctuation. Reading and listening are demonstrated when the story is read by the teacher to the student, and when the student reads alone. Usually, youngsters illustrate their dictated stories, which allows them to interpret their compositions through the medium of art. Dictation, therefore, is an excellent holistic strategy because it is child-focused, process-oriented, and because it interweaves speaking, writing, listening, reading, thinking, and the arts.

Some of the more familiar whole language strategies are listed below.*

Whole Language Strategies

Themes
Listening to literature
Dramatization
Shared reading
Big books
Pattern writing
Personal writing
Personal dictation
Personal dictated sentences
Peer dictation
Storytelling
Readers' theater
Individualized reading
Book talks
Literature dialogue journals
Novel studies
Author studies
Interpretive activities
Reading buddies
Process writing
Writing folder
Written conversation
Writing notebooks
Idea webbing
Word webbing

The role of principals has shifted over the past decade. In addition to being efficient and effective administrators, principals are now expected to be the instructional leaders of their schools. Some research has indicated that principals who teach gain more credibility with their staffs as curriculum leaders than those who don't teach. What implications does this have for principals implementing whole language in their schools?

I agree that principals who work with children in implementing whole language give strong messages of support for teachers to do the same. During the year that I was a half-time teacher and administrator, I attempted the dual role of implementing whole language in my sixth-grade

*This list may be made into an overhead transparency for a staff or parent workshop.

classroom and promoting it in my school. Initially I feared that if I weren't successful in the classroom, my role as curriculum leader would lose credibility, so I shared only my successes at first. The teachers were mildly receptive. However, the staff's attitude became dramatically empathic when I shared some problems I was encountering at one of our in-school networking sessions. I had found that the forty-minute rotary time slot simply wasn't long enough for writing process. One or two of my students wrote only minimally during the writing time; one student still couldn't choose a piece of literature to suit her interest; a parent was stirring up the neighborhood against my program; and the parent in-service program I had initiated flopped! As I reflect on the teachers' reactions I wonder why they were more empathic toward my problems than my accomplishments. Was it my acknowledgment that implementation is not easy? Were they supportive because they too were wrestling with the same issues? Had they recognized how difficult it was for me to let them know that implementing whole language wasn't completely a bed of roses? If I could risk sharing some of the obstacles I was encountering perhaps they could risk sharing their problems. Had my experience helped unite administration and staff to support a common purpose?

I am not advocating that principals teach whole language in order to successfully implement it in their schools. It is simply unrealistic to expect administrators to do so. But I *am* suggesting that principals work in classrooms with their teachers, use whole language strategies with youngsters whenever they can, and listen to teachers' concerns and share in the solving of problems. It is also not necessary for principals to have an in-depth understanding of all the whole language strategies. Their role is to support teachers in whole language instruction.

The whole language strategies discussed here describe each strategy rather than the detailed "how to" information given to teachers. This section is intended to support principals in identifying the key whole language strategies already in use in their schools and to recognize the strategies yet to be implemented.

Many whole language strategies are not new. Teachers have been using some of them for years, and it is important to point these out. For example, teachers are using whole language when they organize their language activities thematically; when they invite the youngsters to dictate complete stories that are written down and read back to the children; when children engage in choral reading (now called shared reading); when students listen to quality literature at storytime or at listening centers; when youngsters engage in problem-solving sessions; when students role-play, create puppet plays, are involved in readers' theater, or when they dramatize stories; and when students engage in interpretive activities at learning centers. Some of the more recent whole language strategies include process writing, shared reading, literature-based individual reading, written conversation, and peer dictation.

Whole Language Strategies Explained

The most common whole language strategies are:

Themes   Natural integration of listening, speaking, reading, and writing occurs through thematic units where the literature selections, shared reading activities, and interpretive activities all relate to a common theme. Themes can be limited to language arts content or can integrate other subject areas, such as mathematics, environmental studies (science, social studies, history, geography), music, art, or physical education.

Listening to Literature   Students in whole language classrooms listen to quality literature (both fantasy and factual) several times a day when the teacher reads to the whole class; a volunteer reads to a small group; reading buddies read to each other; youngsters listen to stories on a video, tape recorder, or record player; and when the principal reads a favorite book to a group.

Dramatization   Dramatization is a natural outgrowth of listening to stories. Young children enjoy **dramatic play** where they spontaneously engage in role-play to depict characters from a favorite story they have heard.

Children of all ages enjoy **moving** to the rhythm of literature by clapping their hands, swaying their bodies, or using rhythm instruments to designate characters or moods in a selection.

Pantomime is an excellent strategy for interpreting meaning of a story as students use all their senses to portray a character from literature accurately.

Role-play situations, where students take on the roles of characters in a story and improvise conversations during particular events, develops a child's comprehension of personality traits of particular characters in a selection.

Interpretive drama—which combines movement, pantomime, role-play, and dramatic play—is a natural extension of literature readings. Interpretive drama also supports comprehension. In order to re-enact the literature, students must have an in-depth understanding of the characters, the setting, and the problems in a story.

Puppet plays provide students with the opportunity to link visual arts with dramatization. Puppets can be made from construction paper taped onto stir sticks, from paper bags, from socks, paper plates, or cloth. The puppeteers can mime the story as a narrator reads, or can role-play their characters as they dramatize the story.

Shared Reading Shared reading is a process by which the whole class or small groups participate in a literature selection as it is read to the group by the teacher. Student participation may be clapping to the rhythm; making musical sounds for various characters; holding up puppets as characters are named in the story; making sound effects for animal characters; making mood sounds for happy, gloomy, or sad parts; or moving in a creative way. Students are also encouraged to join in during re-readings when they hear familiar patterns or refrains in the story. Sometimes teachers will read the narration and have students read the refrain; or have an individual read a favorite page alone.

Shared reading selections for youngsters in kindergarten, first grade, remedial, or English as a Second Language class should be predictable. That is, the next events in the story are readily anticipated in the children's minds even before they read the actual text. Several features make texts predictable in this way. Stories that include real experiences that children have already had give them realistic possibilities about what might happen next. Children might identify a familiar story structure (a fairy tale, for example) that gives them the notion of how this kind of story comes together, and therefore ideas about what is likely to happen next. Selections with strong rhythm and rhyme automatically should build in an expectation for language with particular rhythms and sounds. Illustrations that accompany text very often provide visual clues about the next event.

Big Books   The shared reading strategy can be extended into a comprehension activity when youngsters are given a line of text reprinted by the teacher at the top of a large blank page and are then expected to illustrate it using paint, crayon, or cut-and-paste materials. Once the story has been illustrated, the children reorganize it in the appropriate story sequence, bind it, and read it again and again.

Often youngsters retell new versions of a particular story by changing the rhyme or the pattern. The teacher copies this new text onto a chart or in a big book so students can illustrate it and create a new big book.

Pattern Writing   Pattern writing is a natural outgrowth of the shared reading process, when teachers use a literature selection and have children brainstorm for alternative vocabulary to create a new story. For example, children can take the pattern from *My Mom Travels a Lot* by Caroline Feller Bauer ("the good thing about it is _____; the bad thing about it is _____"), and change it to a pattern story about skating, swimming, holidays, or riding a bike.

Personal Dictation

The personal dictated story is a complete narration either autobiographical or fictional that a student recounts orally while an adult or peer writes it down in the storyteller's presence. Storytelling topics are student chosen and usually result from real happenings, or are reconstructed stories from literature selections students have either heard or read. One student composes the whole story, but during the storytelling the teacher may encourage a more lengthy account by asking questions like: What happened next? Or, Tell me more about that. How did you feel when that happened? The adult or peer prints the story into a student booklet and then reads it back to the student, while pointing to each word. With beginning readers students and teacher read the story co-operatively, allowing the student to take the lead while the teacher fades in and out to maintain the fluency of the reading. Next, the youngster reads alone so that the teacher can observe his or her reading strategies. These would include meaningful story reconstruction (the oral rereading retains the same meaning as the printed text), the use of context strategies (meaning of the story), the use of syntax (the patterns in the text), or left to right finger pointing. Noting and commenting about the composition of the story—such as indicating the most exciting episodes, the quantity of details, the sequence of events, and the interesting language used—will encourage oral story development in the future. The student has the choice of illustrating the story. When students have dictated a particularly enjoyable tale, teachers will often reprint it or make it into published form for peers to read.

Format for Dictated Stories Provide a scrapbook or newsprint booklet for each child in which dictation can be recorded. It could be a scrapbook or teacher-made booklet.

Figure 2.1
Dictation Book

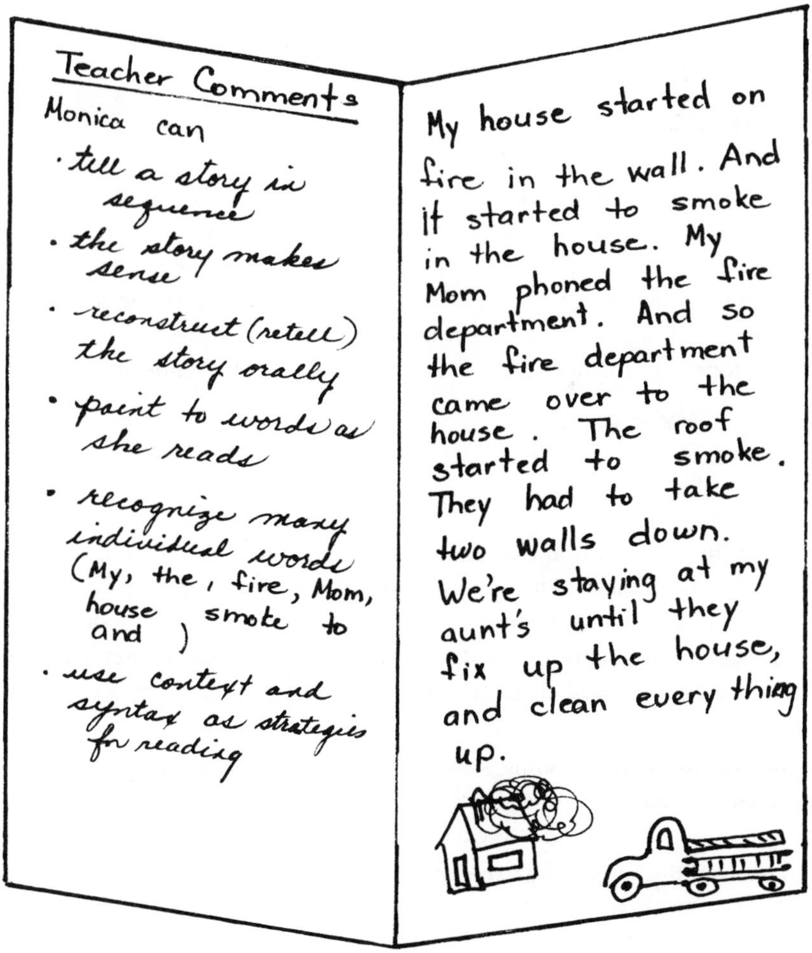

Personal Dictated Sentences

This strategy is useful only for kindergarten and first grade students who are emergent or beginning readers. In this process students are encouraged to tell a story and then to focus on one important aspect and dictate a single sentence. The teacher prints the sentence onto a strip of paper approximately 24" by 6" or 60cm by 15cm, then points to each word as the sentence is read back to the student. Next the child reads the sentence alone, while the teacher observes emergent reading behaviors (directionality, word pointing). The student develops fine motor control and handwriting skills as he or she copies the teacher's text with a colored crayon, pencil, or marker, or copies the same sentence right under the teacher's original.

Peer Dictation

Peer dictation is a whole language strategy especially useful at grades three to six. In this process students work with a partner. One student tells a story, while the partner writes it down. In this way the storyteller can concentrate on the composition of the story while the scribe addresses the handwriting, spelling, punctuation, usage, and grammar. Both can work together collaboratively to revise and edit the composition.

Storytelling

Storytelling is a natural extension of dramatization, shared reading, and personal dictation. Young children can retell stories that have been read to them or that they have heard at the listening center. Older students can read stories by themselves and choose favorites to retell. They can use puppets, flannelboard characters, or props to assist their presentations.

Readers' Theater

In readers' theater small groups of students dramatize a favorite literature selection, while they read particular parts of the story aloud and portray the characters. Usually the story is rewritten as a play by students or adults, and students hold the script as they collaboratively plan, rehearse, and present the play. This is a wonderful whole language strategy to use once students have begun to read.

Individualized Reading

Students in kindergarten to grade six need individual reading experiences as well as shared reading. A book corner where students can select books of their choice can be set up, and scheduled time for students to browse, look at, and read books in a book corner filled with both fiction and nonfiction selections can be provided. Students may share favorite selections with peers at small-group reading conferences where teachers monitor student growth in comprehension and literature appreciation.

Book Talks

Book talks can be conducted by primary, middle-grade, and upper-level students. Initially students may just describe what the book is about. Gradually they may be expected to share a particular aspect they appreciated, such as how a character was described, how a setting was developed, or how the story was structured. Readers eventually begin to note strategies and techniques authors use that young writers may experiment with in their own compositions, such as interesting lead paragraphs, realistic dialogue, detailed events, descriptive settings, and surprise endings.

Literature Dialogue Journals

These are very useful for teachers and students to help them develop an appreciation for varieties of literary genre and for certain authors. Students are encouraged to write about the literature they are reading, to give honest reactions and comments on particular parts they enjoyed or that had special meaning for them personally. Spelling and grammar are not corrected. The teacher usually responds in writing to students, as well as by commenting on another book that the author has written, or by mentioning a book that may elicit a similar emotional reaction.

Novel Studies

Students in kindergarten to grade six enjoy novel studies, which occur in a small group or when the whole class is involved in studying a single novel. The novel may be read to students by the teacher. Sometimes the novel is read by the students themselves. Students have discussions about the work, look at its structure, and respond to interpretive activities related to it.

Author Studies

All grades from kindergarten to grade six enjoy learning about authors. Teachers collect several works from a single author. Teachers of kindergarten and first grade will read the stories to the youngsters, while in grades two to six the students may read the stories themselves. Then the youngsters discuss the characteristics of a particular author with regard to format, structure of stories, intended audience, illustrations, type of genre, etc.

Interpretive Activities

Interpretive activities are important for students in kindergarten to grade six. Youngsters need opportunities to interpret the literature they read or hear through varieties of other media such as writing, drama, puppet plays, mural-making, cut-and-paste, painting, etc. Teachers can provide interpretive opportunities in activity areas, such as listening centers, visual art corners, reading nooks, writing tables, and puppet theaters.

Many teachers develop charts listing general activities. See Table 2.1 for example.

Table 2.1
General Activity Chart

Oral Language Activities

With a friend do a role-play about two characters from the story.
Retell the story using puppets or props.
Discuss how the characters solved the problem in the story. How would you have resolved the issue?
Make up a T.V. commercial to advertise the book.
Make up a puppet play about the story.

Creative Art Activities

Paint a scene from a favorite part in the story.
Make a puppet of a favorite character.
Make a cut-and-paste picture of a character.
Draw four major events in the story.
Paint a mural depicting several key episodes in the story.
Construct a home, vehicle, or object used in the story.

Writing Activities

List some descriptive phrases this author used in the selection.
Write a new ending to the story.
Write a letter to the author.
Write a readers' theater script from this story.
List some personality traits of the character in the story.

Reading Buddies

An excellent whole language strategy that teachers have used for many years is combining an older group of students with a younger class for story readings, personal dictation, or shared writing experiences. Students may read stories to each other; or older students may record personal dictated stories from the younger children; or both may share other stories they have written.

Process Writing

Process writing emphasizes five key processes in writing: idea production, writing, revising, editing, and publishing (see Figure 2.2).

Figure 2.2
Process Writing

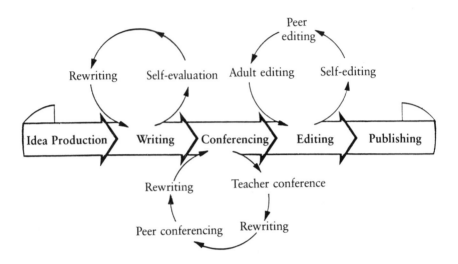

Idea Production   Ideas for writing may result from the act of writing, from peer brainstorming, or from reading and listening to some good literature, as well as from significant experiences students have had.

Writing   In the process of writing students are encouraged to read their own works, taking on the role of audience for compositions written by others. After hearing students read, the authors may expand the concepts or abandon them for different topics and begin again.

Conferencing   Students, as well as the teacher, get involved in responding to student-authored writing by sharing what they liked about the piece and asking questions about parts they don't understand or want to know more about.

Revising   Students decide whether or not changes will be made to the writing contents, by adding more information, expanding a section, reorganizing the ideas for impact, or deleting unimportant ideas.

Editing When students appear satisfied with the selections, content editing begins. Students are invited to edit first, making any obvious corrections and circling other possible errors, questionable spellings, and questionable usage before a team of peers edits the work. Finally, an adult (parent or teacher) edits the writing before it is published.

Publishing Students may plan how their pieces will be published by specifying illustrations; deciding the amount of print for each page; selecting the size of the book; choosing the kind of print desired (hand or type); developing a title page, foreword, information about the author; and attaching an appropriate cover to the finished copy. Once the book is complete, a loan card is placed in it, and it is put into the classroom library corner so other classmates can read it. Not all students want to publish. Many will want their books displayed on the wall or will simply share their final copies with a small group.*

Writing Folder

In this process students write on loose paper and store their drafts in a folder. Completed stories may be placed in a separate compartment of the file. The writing folder can be made from bristol board, from old file folders, or from accordian files. Teachers should have many sizes and shapes of paper available for drafts. Newsprint is a wise choice for initial drafts because it is inexpensive, but other types of paper work well too. Final copy is usually typed on or printed on quality paper for display.

An initial draft may be stimulated by a diary entry, the desire to write a letter to grandma, or the wish to write a folk tale. Once students have completed a first draft they reread it and make a decision at the end of each writing session to leave the writing as is, continue to work on it next

---

*The writing process is *not* linear, however, in that the starting point may not be an idea. Some authors get their ideas after they have begun writing, after listening to a classmate's story during a conference, or after reading a good book. Students should not be required to revise and edit all pieces. In fact, much of a student's writing will remain in first draft form; students revise and edit only those pieces that are important to them.

day, or change topics. Many writing efforts are left at a first-draft stage. Only those pieces the author is committed to are redrafted to final copies. The teacher or student may initiate an interview with a teacher, peer, or small group of peers to share a story and seek reactions and suggestions, but it is the student who decides whether to revise the story (add to it, delete, reorder parts, etc.) for publication.

Students can use the outside of the folder to note possible writing topics and to comment on their personal growth in writing. Teachers can use a section of the folder to comment on developing progress in revision strategies, editing skill, and mechanics (see Figure 2.3).

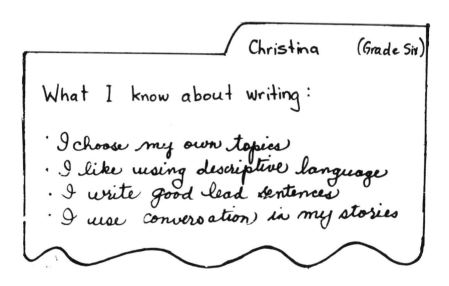

extra topic ideas
self-evaluation
teacher comments
growth in conventions

Written Conversation

A written conversation—a conversation between two people written down rather than spoken—is a popular writing activity for students in

Figure 2.3
Developmental Record-Keeping

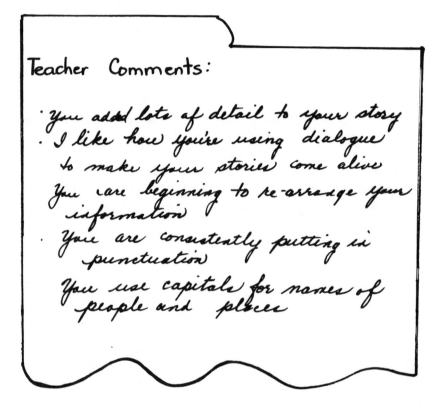

Teacher Comments:
- You added lots of detail to your story
- I like how you're using dialogue to make your stories come alive
  You are beginning to re-arrange your information
- You are consistently putting in punctuation
  You use capitals for names of people and places

grades four to six. Have students work in pairs and give each pair pencil crayons or markers of a different color and one piece of paper. Student A initiates the conversation by writing something in red to Student B. Then Student B continues the written conversation using a black pencil. Several entries are made before students end the conversation.

Students can come up with their own discussion topics but some the teacher may suggest are:

chores at home
homework
bus trips
bullies

violence on T.V.
organized sports

Another form of written conversation involves teachers and students when the teacher responds to a youngster's writing by commenting or questioning some :tem to which the student responds.

Writing Notebooks

Writers of all ages can benefit from a writing notebook. Some teachers use this as a diary or journal, asking students to make daily entries about events that have significance to their lives. I prefer the notebook to be used for first-draft entries of a story; jotting observations of real-life situations that could be incorporated into future stories; documenting remembered impressions, feelings, and visual details of particular personal happenings; and recording interesting examples of description in the literature students are reading.

Idea Webbing

Idea webbing is a good problem-solving, co-operative learning strategy useful in both informational and creative writing for students in kindergarten to grade six. The teacher may record student responses for primary age children, but students in grades three to six can record their own. When students are determining specific areas of a particular subject on which to do research they can start by brainstorming for all the possibilities. For example, a group of students may want to learn more about transportation. The word "transportation" will be placed in the middle of a chart and the youngsters will brainstorm for all the aspects they want to know about, while the teacher or group recorder writes down the possibilities. Then each student chooses a particular area that interests him or her to investigate further (see Figure 2.4).

Word Webbing

Word webbing is also useful in developing alternative descriptive language. A student may want some words to create a spooky mood, and works with a partner or group in developing possibilities (see Figure 2.5).

Figure 2.4
Idea Webbing

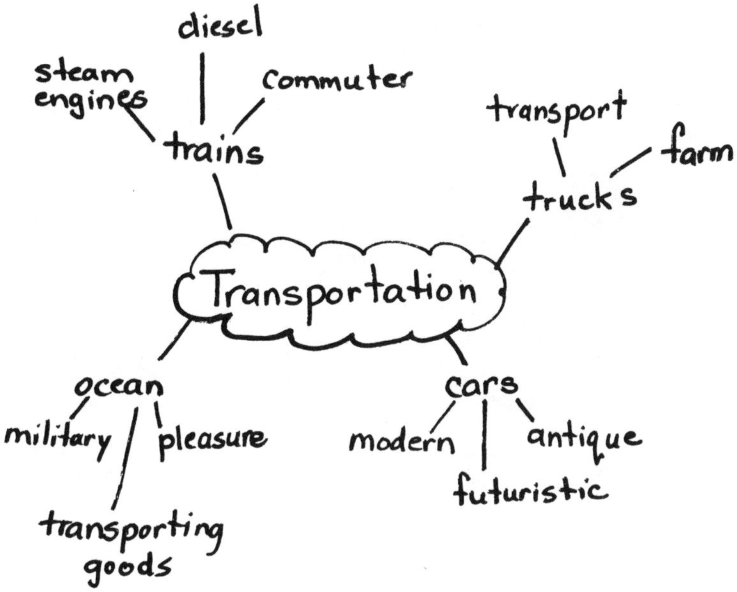

Figure 2.5
Word Webbing

3. Common Questions about Whole Language

Change is not easy for teachers and parents, and since the whole language approach challenges many of our traditional classroom practices in language instruction, teachers and parents will be reluctant to alter their views unless they are assured that language will be learned at least as effectively as it is with skills-based approaches. They will be concerned about the learning of phonetics, spelling, grammar; how to find whole language student materials; how to evaluate. Teachers may begin to ask questions as they speak with colleagues over coffee, at staff meetings, and to you, the administrator, directly. Encourage the questions because they demonstrate that teachers have begun to consider the possibility of whole language. You may feel comfortable fielding the questions yourself. If not, call in your language arts consultant or a whole language expert to respond to the questions that are being raised.

There seem to be some typical questions that teachers and parents ask, and I have prepared responses to some of these queries. You might consider using these questions and answers in a number of ways:

The questions alone could motivate a staff discussion
The staff could come up with their own responses to the questions
The staff might work in pairs to discuss a single question
Staff members might consider doing research on a question from the professional literature
The questions and answers could be redrafted to reflect the specific concerns of your staff.

You might also find the question and answer information handy when responding to parental questions. Consider discussing these queries with parents on curriculum nights or during interview sessions to help them gain an understanding of whole language.

Questions about Philosophy

1. Teachers and parents often ask how students can learn to read by reading. How does that really happen?

    Primary school students learn to *read* in the process of interacting with a meaningful text. This happens when they:

    listen to stories read to them

    participate in choral speaking sessions

    read along with an adult or peers

    choral read (read in unison) poetry, skipping jingles, songs, or predictable literature

    read their own compositions, such as group charts or individual dictated stories

    practice reading independently, matching an oral story to pictures of printed text in their attempt to gain meaning

    reread their own written compositions or peer published materials

    read print in the environment, such as logos on cereal boxes, or print on lunch boxes, on highway signs, on school buses, etc.

    Older students read Trade books and in small groups discuss the concepts and main ideas in these books and analyze their selections for descriptive language, character development, setting, plots, and resolutions.

2. That sounds good, but what about phonics, word study, and spelling?

    In primary school classes phonics and vocabulary understanding are very important aspects of the reading and writing processes. In whole language phonics and vocabulary study are dealt with in the context of reading and writing rather than as isolated skills. The whole language approach also promotes the use of phonics in the writing process in kindergarten and first grade, when youngsters attempt to match phonetic symbols with the oral language sounds of the message they are composing. Beginning spellers really work at phonetics to produce their stories. "I wt s L nt (I went swimming last night)" took Sean more than twenty minutes to write because he labored over each sound (went . . . wu, wu, wu, w; tu, tu, t; swimming . . . s s s; last . . . , L, L, L; night . . . n, n, n, nt.) This sort of meaningful writing activity makes phonics really functional. In the reading process many students do not rely on phonetic strategy initially but rather attempt to make sense of the passages by using picture clues, holistic remembering (approximate recall of the total story), context clues (relying on the meaning of the text for vocabulary clues), or syntax (the usual grammatical order of the sentence).

    Older students in grades three to six learn vocabulary through the process of reading quality books, and in discussions about the descriptive language authors of literature use. Spelling grows as students use quality vocabulary in their own compositions.

3. What kind of reading materials are used in the whole language approach?

Ideally, children's literature selections form the basis of the program, but student-created materials, such as dictated stories or written compositions, are used as well. There are only a few basal publishing companies which include literature selections for beginning readers. Consequently teachers must rely on their school and public libraries for suitable selections.

4. How can students learn to write by writing? Don't they have to have some instruction in letter formation, vocabulary, phonetics, spelling, and grammar before they attempt writing?

Primary school students in the whole language approach can begin to write on the first day of school when teachers allow, accept, and encourage them to write personal thoughts, notes, letters, cards, and stories. They can do so providing they are allowed to represent their compositions through pictures, marks, and scribble. Writing is composing messages, and youngsters can tell stories at the age of three, but they have difficulty with conventional symbolic representation (conventional letters) and spelling. Since the teacher cannot always be the scriber or recorder, students are expected to use their own invented representations to "write" their stories. When they read back their pictures and scribbles we are invited into their world of symbols, and because they see conventional text everywhere—on signs, labels, in their dictated stories, as well as in the literature stories we read to them several times a day—they gradually integrate into their writing the symbols from their particular cultures. Consequently, their writing gradually evolves from temporary to conventional form. That is how writing activities can begin at once, even *before* students have knowledge of phonetics or words.

Older students in grades three to six learn spelling, grammar, and usage during the process of writing. Spelling ability grows proportionately to the amount of writing in which students engage. Spelling, grammar, and usage are further refined when students edit their own stories and those of their peers. When needed, students receive individual and small-group lessons on these conventions.

5. What is meant by real language activities, or real language interactions?

Real language activities involve a complete language event, such as reading a storybook which conveys a whole message and leaves us with something to think about. It may also stimulate further reading, or invite interpretation through art, drama, or movement. Other real language activities include personal dictation; discussion and interaction of ideas among many individuals; or writing a complete story, poem, or research report. Activities in language workbooks *not* considered "real" are isolated phonic drills, letter recognition exercises, or grammar skills.

6. How are listening, speaking, reading, and writing integrated in whole language classrooms?

In primary school classrooms integration of listening, speaking, reading, and writing is promoted in many language strategies outlined in the whole language approach. In the shared reading process, for example, students *listen* to a literature selection, while the adult *reads,* and may read along in unison before they *discuss* (speak) what the story is about and the ideas in it. They may be invited to *compose* (write) a new story based on an idea in the literature, or interpret the story through art or drama. In this instance listening, speaking, reading, and writing are integrated through the shared reading process. Other strategies which naturally integrate listening, speaking, reading, and writing, in addition to the shared reading process, are individual dictation, read-aloud literature sessions, choral speaking, pattern writing, creative writing, drama, and interpretive language activities at the various centers (reading corner, listening center, puppet theater, and construction center).

In grades three to six integration of language occurs when students engage in center activities (listening; speaking; reading; writing; art; construction related to a literature theme, such as friendship, adventure, small creatures, etc.). Integration also occurs when students discuss or write their reactions to the literature they have read, or interpret literature through storytelling, drama, or art.

7. How can language growth be observed? Wouldn't it be better to use pre-tests and post-tests?

Language growth can be observed in students in kindergarten to grade six, but it is a relatively new strategy for classroom teachers who have previously relied on standardized tests for evaluation. Research suggests documenting what we see students doing as they participate in real language experiences, and observing their growth over time. The Whole Language Behavior Inventory (see page 128) lists many actual behaviors of students as they are engaged in listening, speaking, reading, and writing. Standardized tests are not reliable tools for language evaluation because they usually test the student's knowledge of sub-skills (phonetics, letter recognition) and vocabulary out of context with the reading and writing processes. Because they focus on reading almost exclusively, they are not appropriate tools for determining a student's development in other areas, such as listening, speaking, or composition writing. Standardized tests also fail to measure a student's appreciation of literature and knowledge of authors, nor do they measure the desire to read and write. (Refer to section on Evaluation, page 109.)

8. Can holistic strategies be integrated into a skills program?

In the primary grades it is wise to continue some of the strategies with which teachers are comfortable while gradually integrating some holistic strategies which appeal to them. For example, encourage them to try some shared reading strategies and big book activities; both teachers and students will delight in this process. Also invite teachers to consider individual dictation occasionally, especially with some beginning readers, while observing their growth. Suggest they start some daily writing once or twice a week, and increase the time for writing when they see the enjoyment of their students and the growth in composition development. Allow teachers to go slowly, trying one new strategy at a time and not incorporating a new one until they feel comfortable with the old one.

In grades three to six encourage teachers to work with their favorite basal, but to use only selections which have merit and which interest their students. Invite teachers to replace some of the skills activities in the basal with more interpretive activities, such as art, discussions, debates, problem-solving, readers' theater, research, and storywriting. Support them in incorporating a block of time for writing at least three times a week. (Refer to "Making the Transition," page 83.)

9. How do students adjust when they are promoted from a holistic classroom to a skills classroom?

The growth of whole language in a school setting is usually a gradual process. It is rare for a whole staff to adopt it simultaneously. However, over the course of a few years whole staffs have made the transition from skills approaches to whole language when they see the first-hand benefits of the approach. It is quite common that students moving from a whole language setting to a skills setting positively influence receiving teachers when they notice that whole language students appreciate literature, know authors, like to read and write, and tend to be creative thinkers and independent workers. Teachers soon discover that students from whole language classrooms have also experienced a greater volume of reading material, have a broader knowledge of vocabulary, and have more awareness of language processes than skills-based educated students. Those from a whole language classroom are able to integrate the skills of grammar, phonetics, and mechanics into the process of reading and writing better than students from skills programs. Teachers also note that students from whole language classrooms *choose* to read literature, and write for personal enjoyment in school and as leisure activity at home.

Questions about Literature-Based Programs

1. Where is literature found for the whole language approach?

There was a time when children's literature was scarce. However, over the past years the quality and quantity of children's literature has increased dramatically to beyond 400,000 different selections. School and public libraries probably have enough quality selections to get you started. Then you can gradually request specific titles or authors which are appropriate for your grade levels. Teachers are encouraged to choose stories suitable for listening, as well as independent reading. Invite everyone to hunt for selections (parents, teachers, school and public librarians, the students). Choose a variety of genre with interesting texts, which capture children's imaginations, have descriptive language, and appeal to both emotion and intellect. Check in the picture-book section of the school and public libraries and look for authors such as: Martha Alexander, Margaret Wise Brown, John Burningham, Eric Carle, Mirra Ginsburg, Pat Hutchins, Robert Kraus, Mercer Mayer, Robert Munsch, Charlotte Zolotow for children in the primary grades. Judy Blume, Betsy Byars, Beverly Cleary, Robert Cormier, Roald Dahl, Paula Danziger, Lois Duncan, Johanna Hurwitz, Steven Kellogg, Farley Mowat, Katherine Patterson, Cynthia Voigt, and Paul Zindel are popular authors for students in grades three to six. Most school and public libraries will have many of these selections.

2. Isn't it expensive getting class sets of literature selections?

Yes, it would indeed be expensive to obtain class sets of individual selections, but teachers don't have to do this. Groups of students can share one selection when it is made into a big book by reprinting and enlarging the original text on big sheets of paper. In grades three to six, individual selections are mainly used. However, for novel studies, sets of ten should be purchased. Teachers will need five to ten different sets for the year.

3. What role do basal readers play in the whole language approach?

The basal reader can complement the whole language approach, but the issue is "what kind of basal?" Many basals in North America are *not* literature-based but are focused on letter sound, single words, and skills instruction in isolation and provide only non-language text in the early pre-primers, of the "Cat Sat on the Mat" variety. Such basals are in conflict with holistic learning. Literature-based basals, which incorporate literature selections at the earliest levels, support whole language learning. Look for them and consider purchasing them for your teachers. (Refer to "Checklist for Basals," page 89.)

4. How is vocabulary taught in the whole language approach?

For primary school children, learning and extending of literary vocabulary is valued in the whole language approach, but the process by which this occurs differs from traditional approaches. In whole language it is recommended that teachers do not pre-teach the words nor dwell on word learning in the initial stages, because it is believed that students naturally become aware of directionality, story, pattern phrases, and sentences prior to paying attention to the word unit (whole to part learning). Experience has demonstrated that when students share many predictable literature selections in repeated shared reading sessions, they gradually begin to recognize high frequency words within the context of favorite stories quite naturally, and without pre-teaching. Teachers are encouraged to observe students. Once students begin to notice names in stories and high frequency words such as "to, the, got, went, and," and begin to ask what these words are, word recognition grows quickly and naturally without formal word teaching.

For students in grades three to six, vocabulary is learned in the context of reading the story. After the story is read, discussions take place to identify unusual language the author has chosen to use in creating mood, character, or plot. Young authors are encouraged to use this kind of vocabulary in their written stories.

5. What about word banks?

In early primary school classrooms, kindergarten to first grade, word banks can be somewhat useful providing the vocabulary has originated from within meaningful stories. Word banks can also be an outcome of student-dictated sentence strips. Once students recognize complete sentences from several sentence strips these can be cut up, stored in a word bank, and reassembled into meaningful sentences, mixing and matching vocabulary from the original dictated sentences. Collecting words for the purpose of word drill or evaluating early reading has little value.

For older students in grades three to six word banks are inappropriate. However, developing a classroom thesaurus could be very useful for creative writing.

6. How can reading be evaluated when vocabulary counts and basal reader levels are not used?

In primary school whole language classrooms teachers are trained to observe the learning behaviors of students in the act of reading. These documented behaviors listed in the Whole Language Behavior Inventory can be a guide for teachers beginning the whole language process, so that student growth can be monitored. The focus is on print awareness and comprehension rather than word counts and basal levels.

For older students in grades three to six literature-based basals can still be used as benchmark guidelines, remembering that reading a few interesting selections is more valuable than consuming a whole reader. Teachers should be reminded that readability grade levels vary from publisher to publisher and are not consistently reliable.

7. Are parents concerned when a basal is not used?

Yes, initially. But once parents see how excited children are as they learn to read and write naturally, they are delighted. This doesn't happen overnight. The program needs to be explained to them. Encourage teachers to invite parents into the classrooms to participate in the process (scribing, reading to students, publishing books). Once they experience the process they become real supporters in the community. Here are ideas for educating parents.

Teachers in primary classrooms can:

tape record groups and individuals reading their big books and dictated stories during the first term. Compare the tapes to readings in the second term.

invite students to "sign out" class big books to take home. Place comment sheets on the cover so parents can share their reactions.

invite small groups of parents into the classroom after school for informal chats about the program.

Teachers of older students can:

tape record some of the literature discussion sessions.

invite parents to read students' journals in which they react to literature they have read.

send writing folders home periodically so parents can enjoy students' writing growth. (Refer to "Whole Language Tips for Parents," page 105.)

Questions about Dictated Stories

1. Aren't dictated stories just the same as language experience?

The dictated story process has very little in common with the language experience strategies practised twenty years ago. Although both dictated stories and the language experience approach record in print children's oral language, the similarities end there. In language experience the teacher initiates the experience about which the children talk, while in the dictated story process children tell about personal experiences they have had at home, in school, and with literature. The language experience charts are a record of communal experience, while in personal dictation a variety of experiences are recorded.

In language experience both the topic and the structure of the composition are controlled by teachers as they guide responses either through questioning or by rephrasing various student contributions. Even when teachers print out the exact language of each student, the composition that results is a disjointed accumulation of sentences that don't necessarily have any connection. Because of the limited size of the chart the sentences of only a few students are used. And the contribution of any one student is often limited to that of a single sentence.

In personal dictation, on the other hand, the student governs the topic and since it is the narration of a single child the composition is often several sentences long, usually has more cohesion than a group chart story, and frequently shows evidence of story characteristics (story settings, characters' feelings, events, and conclusions). Language experience charts are usually limited to informational accounts, while in personal dictation students are encouraged to share story retellings from the literature they have heard or read. In the dictation process, therefore, students experiment with different genre and over time develop expertise in a variety of story structures.

In language experience the teacher does most of the thinking, including the planning of the experience, the type of structure in the chart story, the questioning of students, and the recording of the text. Students wait and watch, participating only when requested to do so by the teacher. In the personal dictation process the student is more proactive in the planning of the story; in choosing the topic, the genre, the events, the detail, the order of the story; and in deciding on the descriptive language. The teacher plays a secondary role, prompting the storyteller and writing down the story.

The purposes of personal dictation and language experience are also very different. Language experience is often used as a method to teach words or as a prerequisite to the writing process. The personal dictated story, on the other hand, develops storytelling as well as speaking skills and oral composing. Recorded stories can be analyzed over time to document oral language growth. When the dictated story is printed by the teacher, individual students become aware of conventional letters, spaces between words, conventional spelling, capitalization, and punctuation for a whole story rather than for a single sentence. Dictated stories also provide students with predictable material to read. But one of the most important aspects of the personal dictated story is that it supports the growth in story composition that lays the conceptual groundwork for writing compositions.

2. Shouldn't the dictated story process terminate once youngsters begin to write for themselves?

Many whole language advocates support this view because they perceive language experience as a prerequisite to writing. They fear that children will build an unhealthy dependency on the teacher to provide handwriting and spelling for them, rather than taking risks in starting to write for themselves. Indeed, some kindergarten and first grade teachers reinforce this dependency by delaying the writing process until youngsters are, in their view, ready to write on their own.

I believe that the personal dictated story should not be a prerequisite to the writing process but should be a parallel process. I advocate that youngsters in kindergarten to sixth grade should simultaneously have opportunities for daily writing as well as weekly dictation, because weekly dictation sessions allow students to concentrate on story composition while someone else is taking care of handwriting, spelling, and conventions. The story therefore develops quickly and fluently because students don't have to stop and deliberate over the spelling of words. Beginning writers especially, in my view, need opportunities for weekly dictation, since they are often frustrated when their grandiose stories— stories they are able to rehearse in their minds or tell to friends—result in only one or two sentences because they must devote so much time and energy to manipulating a pencil and spelling words. The weekly dictated story provides the developing writer with a chance to share a complete story once a week, allowing composition to evolve. At the same time young writers become aware of conventional spelling, punctuation, and grammar modeled in the transcription process, and reinforced for their own writing efforts.

I believe that students benefit from opportunities to dictate personal stories once a week, as well as to write their own stories every day.

3. How is time managed for thirty-five students who want to tell a complete story each day?

In primary school classrooms every student does not participate in individual dictation each day. Ideally, each student does a single individual dictation experience once a week, which means that approximately seven students will dictate a story each day. This may vary depending on the support resources and grade level of students. If the teacher is the only scribe, students may dictate once every *two* weeks. With the use of volunteers, parents, custodians, principal, older students, or peers, *two* dictations per week are possible.

4. Who takes dictation?

School personnel—such as teachers, teacher aides, principals, custodians—make excellent scribes, but volunteers (including parents and grandparents, older students in grades four to six) also do a fine job. Consider a training session for volunteers, and advise them to transcribe in pencil rather than pen until they feel comfortable with the process.

Students in grades three to six enjoy peer dictation once a week, where partners take turns telling a complete story or writing the story down.

5. What happens if a student cannot think of anything to tell?

Sometimes oral prompting may be necessary to assist a student who cannot think of a story. Also consider periodic class brainstorming sessions, and list all the ideas which result from a question such as: "What are you going to write about today?"

It is important that students, rather than the teacher, make the topic choice so that they feel in control and bring their own unique experiences to the dictation process.

6. Once students can read and write, can individual dictation diminish or cease?

Individual dictation is often considered only useful as an early reading and writing activity, but it is exceedingly beneficial to continue the process long after students have begun to read and write on their own. Dictation continues to produce high interest reading material for individuals and classmates; it enhances composition skills; and it is a natural way to share folk tales, reports, and dramatizations.

7. Why is the exact language the student uses recorded in the dictation booklet? Doesn't that reinforce immature language patterns?

It is important that exact language be recorded so that an accurate record of oral language is obtained. From this language sample one can determine the level of speaking, or reveal a speech problem needing appropriate remediation. Over time dictation samples will demonstrate when an oral language difficulty has been overcome. Reading inaccurate language doesn't appear to be reinforcing but rather leads to self-correction. When students read their dictated stories they often exclaim, "That doesn't sound right," and will request alteration.

8. When is incomplete oral language corrected?

Immature language can be modeled through extended conversation. For example, if the child says, "Me go to the store," the teacher can respond, "Oh, you went to the store." At some point the teacher may wish to focus on a single speech problem—the correct use of pronouns, for example. In subsequent dictation students and teachers may work on editing that particular form, but should not move on to another problem until the student begins to self-correct in oral dictation.

9. Aren't dictated stories low quality reading material?

It is true that personal dictated stories are usually of a lower quality of language than that in literature. However, because literature is an integral part of the whole language approach, students who have regular opportunities to dictate often integrate characteristics of literature into their stories. The dictation process is invaluable in learning how to read and in providing high interest predictable text for beginning readers. Dictation is also vital in the writing process because students are free to concentrate only on the composition while the scribe focuses on the mechanics and handwriting. Students benefit from both literature and dictation in a whole language program.

10. How are skills taught in the dictation process?

First we must clarify what is meant by skills. The skills developed in the whole language approach include a sense of story, meaning, holistic remembering, directionality (left to right direction of pages and lines of print), reading-like behavior, prediction skills, and concepts of words and spaces. Skills in vocabulary identification and phonetic awareness follow quite naturally without the need for *formal* instruction.

11. Are sentence strips an outgrowth of the dictated story?

Sentence strips can be initiated from the dictated story, but most often they result from a separate dictation experience or they may result from labeling objects around the classroom (for example, this is the painting corner). Children will also compose sentences based on a sentence pattern they have read in literature.

Questions about Process Writing

1. What is meant by process writing?

Process writing is a term used to describe what all writers do. Students select topics about which they know a lot and write a first draft. Authors then read and reread and make changes in the draft so that communication is clear. Youngsters share this initial draft with student peers who ask questions for clarification. Writers respond by considering areas they might change. Changes in content are made and sharing sessions may be repeated. When authors are satisfied with their pieces, they edit for spelling, punctuation, and grammar; peers edit; and finally adults edit. Then students plan a way to share the work with others.

2. How is writing taught naturally?

In primary school classrooms teachers don't teach writing but students learn to write naturally when teachers:

encourage daily writing

allow students to choose their own topics

accept students' invented symbols in the form of pictures, marks, scribble, invented letters, and spellings to represent the thoughts they wish to communicate

don't rush to correct all mechanics and grammar, but work on one skill at a time considering the developmental stage and the needs of the writer

focus on the learner and the process first, and the written product later
evaluate growth over time.

In grades three to six writing grows naturally when teachers encourage
students to write at least three times a week for approximately forty-five
minutes each time. Teachers can then:

encourage students to choose their own topics

share strategies actual authors use in the literature students read

encourage student authors to share their writings with peers who sensitively
respond

support students in focusing on clarity of communication

celebrate student growth in writing (composition, spelling, and conventions) over time.

3. Don't students need to learn handwriting skills before they can write?

In primary school classrooms there is no need to delay the writing process
until students can manipulate a pencil, since students are able to compose
stories by the age of three. Students can begin composing when they are encouraged to *tell* their stories to an adult scribe (dictation) or communicate
stories through pictures or scribble.

Older students can choose to print, type, or use calligraphy for the print in
their final copies.

4. How is handwriting taught?

In primary school classrooms there is no need to teach handwriting formally.
Students see conventional script everywhere in the classroom environment: on
signs, dictated labels, dictated story charts, and in literature pattern books. In
addition, students note conventional text as they observe scribes recording their
personal stories. Students also practice writing conventional text when they
over-copy or under-copy their dictated sentence strips, as well as in their own
story writing.

5. What about spelling? Doesn't spelling have to be taught and errors corrected
in composition? How else will students learn to spell?

For students in kindergarten to grade six spelling is an important aspect of
writing, but focusing on formal instruction and correction prematurely can
actually impede composition and spelling development. Formal spelling programs rarely include actual vocabulary needed in story writing. Many studies
indicate that spelling grows proportionately to the volume of writing produced,
that students naturally have a desire to spell correctly, and that their spelling
ability grows steadily as they spell correctly high frequency words needed in
their compositions, while using temporary spellings for the words they don't
know. A word used more than five or six times in a week, for example, will
likely be one of the first to be spelled conventionally. At individual writing
conferences spelling can be discussed, and the complete spelling of one or two
frequently used words can be taught. But it is important to wait for the transfer
and internalization of knowledge to take place before making a new spelling
suggestion. Editing for publication also heightens spelling awareness.

6. Are students taught to scribble?

In kindergarten and grade one we do not teach our children to scribble. Rather, non-readers are allowed to use invented marks when they have *no* knowledge of conventional letters, sound-symbol relationships, or a sight vocabulary. Some kindergarten students, a few first graders, and language-delayed students may rely on scribble behavior, but usually scribble is used for only a few months. It diminishes rapidly once students begin to read and transfer their knowledge of conventional print to written stories.

Older students (unless they are delayed in their ability to write) do not use scribble behavior at all.

7. How are the skills of punctuation and grammar taught?

In kindergarten to grade six classrooms mechanics and grammar are important components of the writing process. Specific lessons are most effective when they reflect the needs of students and when instruction relates to the context of individuals' writing. Consequently, lessons are given in conferences for individuals or small groups. A single convention is the focus until students transfer new learning to written compositions. Writing conventions are further reinforced in the editing and publishing process.

8. Which is more important, creativity or correct form?

For writers in kindergarten to grade six both form and creativity are necessary for good writing. Teachers' concerns for perfection, however, result in focusing on too many form considerations too soon. These may overwhelm young writers, who don't know where to begin and so frequently don't. Creativity and composition should be encouraged first, and perfection of form worked on gradually later.

9. Teachers of grades two to six often ask: Why can't students write when they come into my classroom?

There is no easy answer. Have teachers begin by examining their personal definitions of writing in order to identify the exact behaviors students *can* manage (be sure they consider composition, symbolic representation, spelling, conventions, and attitudes). Encourage teachers to make a collective chart of these positive behaviors, and then further encourage growth in other conventions gradually over the course of the year. This positive approach at least helps to lift teachers' spirits somewhat, since they are focusing on what their students *can* do rather than on their deficits.

10. How should teachers respond to parents who want their children's work corrected all the time?

The school has a responsibility to listen to parents of students with whom they work. Encourage teachers to invite small groups of parents to school for discussions, and listen to parents' expectations as well as sharing teachers' own goals. The group can compile a list of co-operative goals and discuss strategies for meeting them. Have teachers share their students' work so that parents can see actual writing samples over time. Encourage teachers to invite parents to visit the classroom at writing time, and ask some to become classroom volunteers. Once parents have experienced the writing process with students they become as excited by the process as you are, and consequently become ambassadors for this approach in the community.

11. What is done when students limit their stories to only the vocabulary they know how to spell?

These are students who need their confidence strengthened. Encourage teachers to give them many opportunities to *dictate* stories, so that they become aware of their competence in storytelling; convince students that their written stories can be as interesting as their dictation; have students use invented spellings for unknown vocabulary, and assure them that their spelling efforts will be accepted. Once students *really* believe that invented symbols are allowed and valued, they will begin to take some risks in their story writing. It will take time, however.

12. How many books will individual students publish in a year?

This will vary from student to student and classroom to classroom. A few may publish as many as ten books per year; others will only want to publish one; while many students publish five or six books each year. Publishing a final product, however, is not as important as the writing-drafting-revising process.

4. Implementation

THE PRINCIPAL'S ROLE IN IMPLEMENTING
WHOLE LANGUAGE

As we have read, current research indicates that the principal's role is critical for ensuring positive implementation of any school innovation, and it is especially crucial in implementing whole language. For example, principals who have training in implementation processes are more likely to effect successful change (Michael Fullan, 1985; Kenneth Leithwood and Deborah Montgomery, 1986). Such training will increase your knowledge of the change process and enable you to lead whole language implementation in your school successfully. Common stages of most school-based change processes include: reviewing current school practice, setting school goals, providing curriculum resources, developing a school implementation plan, and monitoring growth in implementation. An example of the change process related to whole language is outlined in depth on page 87 of this book.

Principals effective in implementation use collaborative, collegial decision-making styles. You can make whole language implementation a reality when you involve the staff in selecting the innovation they want. Teachers will become more committed to the change process when they are involved in decision-making. Avoid mandating whole language with a staff that is resistant. Instead, work in depth with one or two teachers who indicate an interest, until there is general interest and commitment from the staff as a whole.

Principals who are flexible, pro-active risk-takers and who are problem-solving strategists support positive implementation (Kenneth Leithwood and Mary Stager, 1986). For example, staffs will often try to implement all aspects of whole language during the first year, rather than taking incremental steps. But there is no way of knowing this in advance. So principals who can identify such problems as they emerge, and develop strategies so that the staff can solve them together, will have greater success in implementing whole language.

Implementation success is more likely to occur in schools where principals have created an atmosphere of trust, communication, and interactions; and where experimentation is encouraged and risk-taking is safe (Michael Fullan, 1985; and Kenneth Leithwood, 1982). When teachers are trying out whole language strategies for the first time, they need to know that you support their experimental attempts and that you do not expect perfection in the beginning. When you provide forums for them to share both their successes and failures you demonstrate that risk-taking is safe.

Schools that have success in implementation also have principals who acquire material and consultative resources, arrange for teacher visitations, promote teacher-teacher coaching, and provide non-teaching time so that teachers can attend in-service sessions (Leithwood, 1982; and Susan Showers, 1983a, 1983b). This involves seeking funds from superintendents for whole language resource materials, consultative time, and supplying teachers and professional development funds so that your staff can learn from the whole language experts who are available.

Teachers with whom I have worked across the United States and Canada support implementation research. They say that the principal's attitude, style, and support are crucial to the successful implementation of whole language. They appreciate principals who have discussions with them, share ideas, provide resources, listen to their problems, and work in the classroom with their students. Teachers very often feel alone and wonder if principals really appreciate how hard it is to implement a new process when classrooms are overcrowded, when resources may be limited, when students resist, and when parents are not cooperative. If you really listen to teachers' concerns, acknowledge the realities of the classroom, and attempt to resolve some of their problems, even if it means coming into the classroom yourself and working with the children occasionally, teachers realize that you, too, are willing to take risks and share the implementation challenge with them. Once teachers feel that you and they are working together toward the same shared goal, they are more likely to become committed to implementing whole language.

Teachers also need to know that they have some decision-making power regarding the aspects of whole language they want to implement first, the kind of in-service they prefer, the experts they want to work with, and the materials they'd like to use. It is my experience that the more teachers are actively involved in the implementation decisions, the more committed and involved they become. They also are more willing to actually try new strategies and collectively solve the problems that emerge.

Principal's Checklist for Successful Implementation

The characteristics of principals cited by researchers as having a positive effect on implementation in the school are given in Table 4.1. Rate yourself high if you demonstrate the behavior frequently. A rating of medium indicates that you are aware of the attributes of the characteristic but only sometimes practice it. A low rating indicates that although you may recognize the attribute as being beneficial, you rarely have time to consider the behavior. Should your score be high or medium on at least fifteen of the characteristics you have the potential to effect implementation of whole language in your school positively. But if your score is lower, you may want to proceed cautiously. Regardless of your rating, consider starting an administrative network group interested in whole language implementation, where you can share ideas, strategies, and solutions to obstacles. Share research articles; call in some experts who can provide strategies for administrators; visit a school where a principal has implemented whole language and talk to him or her about successful processes used; consider using that principal as a coach.

SCHOOL-BASED IMPLEMENTATION

The role of the principal in the implementation process has changed dramatically over the past twenty years. Until recently principals have relied on the top-down autocratic model of implementation referred to in the research literature as the technological model. You and your teachers are probably familiar with this approach because it is characterized by having a strong policy base, usually mandated by state departments of education or ministries of education; a development phase, usually in the form of

Table 4.1
Principals' Checklist for Successful Implementation

	Rating		
	High	*Medium*	*Low*
As a principal I can positively affect implementation when I . . .			
focus on and get actively involved in curriculum implementation			
attend all in-service related to the innovation			
am involved in professional reading			
have substantial knowledge of curriculum development, effective instruction, and program issues			
have training in curriculum implementation processes			
have elementary school education and training			
seek advice on important issues			
spend time teaching			
recruit my own staff and assign staff based on curriculum expertise, values, positive staff relations, as well as school needs			
manage time well and develop a balance between and among instructional leadership, routine administration, human relations, and program innovations			
create a climate of collegiality, communication, trust, interaction, technical sharing; for experimentation; on-going staff development; and an atmosphere where risk-taking is safe			
develop and establish strong communciation and relationships with and among teachers, consultants, trustees, administrators (superintendents), and community			
am a flexible, open, risk-taker, pro-active, honest, sincere, fair, encourager of growth, effective strategist			
make myself available as a sounding board for teacher problems and ideas			
believe in, establish, and sustain long-range goals; have high tolerance for diversity of goals			
match school goals to that of the community			

	Rating		
	High	*Medium*	*Low*
develop strategies to clarify and classify problems, prioritize problems, prevent problems, develop clear problem-solving procedures, solve problems collaboratively to reflect on others' problem-solving style			
use collaborative, collegial decision-making, delegate authority, have informal style of authority			
match staff to innovation projects			
promote teacher-teacher coaching			
arrange for in-service that relates to school goals			
gain consultant and material resources			
create an atmosphere that supports experimentation and allows failures			

printed curriculum documents developed by the system rather than school personnel; a diffusion stage, where curriculum documents are delivered to the school door for you to distribute to your teachers; and, finally, the adoption stage, which is assumed, providing teachers have received and read the print materials. The principal's role in this approach is one of delivery of documents and encouragement of their use. Today's researchers claim that the technological model simply doesn't work, and that most educational innovations have never really been truly implemented.

Researchers have identified several factors that contribute to the ineffectiveness of the technological model: It does not accommodate for the fact that change occurs over long periods of time; it negates social interaction and mutual problem-solving between the experts and teachers; it lacks a process orientation; it does not involve principals and teachers in the development of the curricula; it does not allow principals and teachers to have decision-making influence regarding how implementation will take place; it does not design a curriculum that necessarily addresses a particular school need; it does not provide a systematic in-service for a complete staff over time. In spite of the fact that researchers have rejected the technological approach to implementation it is still the most commonly used approach in educational systems across North America.

Current research suggests that implementation will be more successful when the principal takes a strong leadership role in the implementation process in the school. This process involves the principal and staff assessing their school needs; developing a school-identified curriculum focus; locating curriculum materials that suit the school's requirements; developing their implementation plan; planning for their in-service; and evaluating their growth in implementation.

Much of the work on school-based implementation is still at the theoretical stage, but some practical procedures are beginning to emerge that principals can use to guide their staffs in the change process. One such procedure, presently being considered (Michael Fullan, Kenneth Leithwood, Gail Heald-Taylor, 1987) can be used with any curricula, but this example will use whole language.

There are five key phases in this school-based implementation process:

1. planning for change
2. review for initiation
3. development
4. implementation
5. review for continuation.

During the planning phase you will be involved in obtaining central office commitment, enlisting the support of local experts, and gaining background in whole language yourself.

The review for initiation phase involves establishing a school implementation team (SIT), inviting staff support for school-based implementation, generating change possibilities for the benefit of students, developing an awareness of and interest in whole language, and assessing whole language needs in the school.

In the development stage staffs determine their focus, set goals and objectives, find available resources, and locate experts who can assist them in implementing whole language.

At the implementation phase staffs develop a school-based implementation plan according to the needs of the staff, and then proceed with their in-service.

During the final review for continuation phase staffs evaluate their growth both formatively and summatively.

Planning for Change (1 to 10 months)

The success of your whole language initiative is greatly facilitated when commitment is gained from central office staff. It is therefore important that your superintendents support the whole language innovative thrust both in principle and financially. Write up a proposal for a one-to-three-year plan and present it to your superintendent, outlining your goals and some of your potential needs, such as supply teacher time for in-school goal setting, classroom visitations, and professional development activities; funds for staff to attend conferences, as well as for bringing in special speakers; and money for professional resources and student materials.

Share your project with the local language arts consultant as well, and negotiate for his or her time for in-school whole language workshops and demonstration lessons.

You may also decide that you need professional training in whole language or in the curriculum implementation process, and will require professional development funds to do so.

Above all, give yourself time to build up your knowledge in whole language, time to develop an understanding of your leadership role in the curriculum implementation process in the school, and time to develop your own personal strategies for proceeding with schoolwide whole language implementation.

Review for Initiation (1 to 3 Months)

School Implementation Team It is likely that your staff has not been involved in a schoolwide implementation project before, so have a discussion about how school-based implementation works; and how it maximizes teacher involvement, student needs, and staff decision-making. Consider sharing with the staff an overview of the process, or call in an expert in implementation to do this for you.

Establish a small staff group to form a school implementation team (SIT) which is to facilitate the process in future sessions by leading discussion groups, planning in-service sessions, collecting data, and developing implementation plans. The SIT works most effectively if its members represent a cross-section of grades and curriculum expertise.

Awareness of Change Possibilities   Teachers are often not aware of the need for change. They have developed instructional strategies over the years that seem to work for them, and see no reason to try something new. There are several strategies you can use to develop an awareness of change toward whole language.

I prefer to take advantage of the natural events that happen on any staff. A teacher returns from a conference on whole language bursting with enthusiasm, so invite that teacher to share the experience at a staff meeting. Another teacher has begun to use some shared reading strategies as the result of a consultant's visit; put some of the big books on display in the hall. Post on the bulletin board some recent articles you have read on whole language and place a few photocopies on the staff-room table so teachers can borrow them. At budget time discuss with teachers why they are ordering class sets of phonic workbooks and invite them to use their budget funds for literature selections instead. After a teacher observation session in a classroom where process writing is being initiated, set up a display case of student published books.

You can also use some other pro-active strategies. For example, set up a staff-room display of articles and books using staff-selected articles as well as professional materials you have read, and use books listed in the resource section of this book (see page 162). Leave the display up for two or three weeks and observe what the staff does. Do they ignore the material? Do they start to pick it up and read it? Do you hear informal discussions about it? Do teachers argue about the articles?

Send one or two staff members to a whole language conference and have them report back to the staff. Encourage a staff member to visit another school where whole language is practiced, and have a buzz session at recess. At a staff meeting initiate a discussion about whole language. You might start the session by saying something like: "I'm hearing and reading a lot about whole language lately and wondered what you think about this approach?" Listen to the responses and record the comments, questions, and concerns that arise. Share your personal commitment to literacy with your staff, and encourage teachers to discuss what they think.

Awareness of Whole Language   Once some general awareness has been informally provided, discuss openly with the staff the idea of pursuing whole language as a schoolwide curriculum. If the staff as a whole is more resistant than interested in whole language at this time, it is better to delay schoolwide implementation until their interest increases. In the meantime, continue to support the two or three teachers who are keen about whole language by providing them with the resources they need, such as literature selections, listening centers, and writing materials. Invite system consultants to provide workshops and classroom demonstrations. Support school networking sessions for this small group so they can share strategies, resources, and solve problems together. If at all possible, provide some in-school time for these sessions. Encourage these teachers to visit each others' classrooms and other schools that are using whole language. Make these teachers aware of conferences, guest speakers, and workshops that relate to whole language, and negotiate funds from the central office so they can attend.

If staff members indicate an interest in whole language, proceed through the stages of this implementation process. Begin by simply having an informal discussion about whole language and have the SIT record the various comments and questions. Issues that usually emerge from such a discussion are: What is the philosophy of whole language? How is it different from what we are already doing? What's wrong with skills-based approaches? What are the principles of whole language? What are the key whole language strategies? What about evaluation? What do parents expect?

These questions are valuable in providing information for future planning. For example, the SIT could find some articles that would respond to the questions; they could draw teachers' attention to the various sections in this book, such as the outline of the philosophy of whole language (see page 4), the comparison between skills-based and whole language approaches (see page 13), the common questions asked about whole language (see page 37), and the section on evaluation (see page 109).

Consider inviting a consultant to talk about what whole language is, to show the staff a video or a tape-slide presentation, or to encourage teachers to visit another school or other colleagues' classes where whole language is being used.

The intent of these presentations and visits is to develop an awareness only of the principles and features of whole language. A deeper understanding will come over time, once teachers begin to use the strategies with their students.

Whole Language Characteristics   After the staff has seen a media presentation of whole language, or visited a whole language classroom, have teachers brainstorm in small groups to list the characteristics of whole language that they saw on the video or during a classroom visit. You may decide to invite your language arts consultant to this session to ensure that the key aspects of whole language get on the chart. A typical chart may look like Figure 4.1.

Figure 4.1

Characteristics of a Whole Language Classroom

- there's a lot of talking
- the students work together a lot
- there are many activity centers
- students choose their own literature
- students write almost every day
- students seem to work well together

Areas of Change   From the lists of characteristics organize items under some key headings. For example, students talking and making decisions could go under the heading of problem-solving; the book corner, writing table, sand-and-water stand could go under the heading of centers. Then, develop one chart showing the major aspects involved in whole language. The chart might contain the items in Figure 4.2.

ASSESSING A WHOLE LANGUAGE SCHOOL

Before your staff begins to implement whole language systematically you may encourage them to share information about their present language programs in view of whole language philosophy. This information will help you to determine your school implementation needs. For example, you may discover that teachers are practicing very few whole language

Figure 4.2

> # Whole Language Strategies
>
> - daily reading to
>   children
> - shared reading
> - reading corner
> - personal dictation
> - written conversation
> - diary writing
>
> - centers
> - drama
> - problem-solving
> - writing folders
> - conferencing
> - revising
> - holistic evaluation

strategies and have strong beliefs in skills-based philosophy. Or you may find that most of your teachers are using literature-based programs and are beginning to involve their students in process writing. Each situation requires different implementation strategies. In the first example implementation may focus on changing the beliefs of the staff, while efforts in the second example would probably concentrate on changing teachers' classroom practices.

It will be important to clarify to your staff that the purpose of collecting this information is to provide data to support implementation decisions for the school regarding what areas of whole language to implement first, what staff strength is available for teacher-teacher coaching, and to determine what the need is for out-of-school resource support. Be aware that some of your staff may worry that this information will be used to evaluate them as teachers. If that appears to be the case with your staff, invite them to share the information anonymously.

Encourage your staff to be involved in selecting the format(s) for collecting information, so that the individuality of your school will be reflected. Teachers may choose to describe (orally or in written form) their philosophy of language learning and the classroom strategies they use to support their beliefs. They might develop their own format for collecting information about their philosophies, instructional strategies, classroom organization, and evaluation. Outside experts may be called in to work with the staff in developing an inventory of classroom practice. Or they may consider using the Whole Language Assessment Inventory in Table 4.2 (or modifying it) to collect information about whole language practice in the school.

Once the information is collected, the school implementation team (SIT) can analyze the data and report to the staff. Keep this information on file so that at the end of a year the staff can repeat the process and determine the degree of change that has occurred over that time.

Table 4.2
Whole Language School Assessment Inventory

	Ineffective	Somewhat effective	Effective	Very effective
Listening				
How effective is your whole language program in providing for: Opportunities for listening to quality literature read to them by you or a volunteer? Opportunities for listening to quality literature at a listening center? Opportunities to listen to a variety of genre (fantasy and factual)? Opportunities to listen and respond in discussions, on the telephone, in debates?				
Speaking				
How effective is your whole language program in providing for: Opportunities for students to talk? Opportunities for students to discuss? Opportunities for students to dramatize? Opportunities for students to role-play with puppets or on the telephone? Opportunities to argue, debate?				

Opportunities to use social language (introduction, thank yous)?				
Opportunities to dictate personal narrations of more than five sentences?				
Opportunities to give reports?				
Opportunities to engage in co-operative learning with peers?				
Opportunities to be involved in problem-solving sessions?				
Reading				
How effective is your whole language program in providing student opportunities:				
To have quality stories read to them?				
To read environmental print?				
To participate in shared reading activities?				
To participate in dramatizing quality literature?				
To read quality pattern literature?				
For reading a variety of genre (fact, fiction, poetry, narrative, biography, etc.)?				
To dictate a personal narrative of more than five sentences every week?				
To choose selections to read for recreation?				
To read self-selected books for leisure?				
To use a variety of cueing strategies to seek meaning, such as pictures, patterns, tracking (word pointing), memory, context, syntax, and phonetics?				
To study novels?				
To study authors?				
To discuss the meaning of literature in individual or small group conferences?				
To interpret literary selections in a variety of ways (discussion, art, music, drama, writing)?				

	Ineffective	Somewhat effective	Effective	Very effective
Writing				
How effective is your whole language program in providing student opportunities:				
To write for at least 30 to 60 minutes each day (except kindergarten)?				
To choose their own topics for writing?				
To dictate personal and fantasy stories of more than five sentences in length?				
To record stories through retellings, drawings, scribble, invented marks (appropriate only at kindergarten and first grade)?				
To dictate group compositions (letters, lists, charts, poetry)?				
To write every day in a notebook or folder?				
To write according to a model presented by the teacher (pattern story, poetry, letters, folk tale, fable, essay)?				
To write for a variety of purposes (notes, lists, surveying, letters, reports, fiction)?				
To write in many subject areas?				
To experiment with spelling, punctuation, and grammar?				
To work at a writing center?				
To engage in written conversation strategies (grades four to six)?				
For becoming aware of audiences other than themselves?				
To respond to writings of self and others?				
To exchange oral responses to writing of peers?				
To exchange written responses to writings of peers (grades two to six)?				

To participate in teacher conferences?				
To participate in conferences with peers?				
To revise the ideas of a composition by adding more information, rearranging the order, or deleting redundant portions?				
To draft two or more times (grades two to six)?				
To edit their own stories for spelling, punctuation, and grammar?				
To edit stories of peers for spelling, punctuation, and grammar (grades three to six)?				
To work in an editing team (grades two to six)?				
To publish writing in booklets, posters, storyboards, big books, etc.?				
To share a variety of authors?				
Interpretive Activities				
How effective is your whole language program in providing for students:				
Varieties of ways to interpret themes and literature selections such as discussions, art, drama, writing, construction, puppets, etc.?				
Activities that reflect higher level thinking skills?				
To be engaged in co-operative learning situations with small groups?				
To engage in a variety of language-related learning centers such as a book corner, listening post, drama center, construction area, art station, writing table?				
To engage in a variety of learning centers related to other subject areas, such as mathematics, science, environmental studies, music, and physical education?				

	Ineffective	Somewhat effective	Effective	Very effective
Evaluation				
How effective is your whole language program in providing opportunities: For students to evaluate their own growth?				
For students to be involved in peer evaluation?				
To document growth of students in log books?				
To document growth of students on checklists, rating scales, or inventories?				
To document growth through retelling?				
To document growth through samples of work (dictation, writing samples)?				

Development

Whole Language Focus   Since whole language encompasses such a broad area, group your strategies under some global headings (reading, writing, listening, speaking, interpretive activities, evaluation). Then prioritize these areas to determine a single staff focus of study for one year. To facilitate your decision-making, consider criteria such as:

1. the relevancy of the content across grade levels
2. the degree of interest in the topic
3. the degree to which it addresses concerns of parents
4. the benefits to students
5. the effect on other subject areas.

It is also important to use the criteria your staff suggests. By a show of hands record the decisions of the group. The resulting tally should indicate the preference of your staff. Figure 4.3 is a typical decision-making chart. For this, staff writing emerges as the first focus area.

Figure 4.3
Curriculum Focus

Whole language areas	Criteria			
	Grade level relevance	Benefits to students	Interest	Tally
Reading	✓✓ ✓ ✓	✓✓✓	✓✓	9
Writing	✓✓✓✓	✓✓✓✓	✓ ✓✓✓	12
Listening/Speaking	✓ ✓ ✓	✓ ✓	✓	6
Interpretive activities	✓✓✓	✓ ✓	✓	6
Centers	✓✓	✓✓	✓	5
Drama	✓ ✓	✓ ✓	✓	5
Evaluation	✓✓✓	✓✓	✓✓	7

This process will be difficult for teachers because many will believe that they can implement all aspects of whole language at once. They can't see the need for choosing one strategy focus at a time. But trying to implement a massive innovation such as whole language across a school is an overwhelming and complex task. Unless you have unlimited resources and an extremely energetic staff, my advice is to progress gradually with manageable chunks.

You may encounter a situation where the staff as a whole chooses writing as the school focus, but one or two of the staff already feel comfortable in this area. In such a case use these teachers' expertise to support the growth of other teachers and assist such teachers in developing a personal implementation plan that may extend beyond that of the staff's.

It is important to point out that the actual process rarely goes as smoothly as outlined, so come to this first session with a group of experts. You may consider inviting experts in problem-solving processes, a principal and colleagues who have already experienced this phase of implementation, or a consultant knowledgeable in whole language to call on as required.

Expect that this phase could take one or more half-day sessions. After all, the staff is deciding on an implementation focus in which they will be engaged for one or two years, so expect an outpouring of honest comments and legitimate questions that will have to be addressed before the staff will feel comfortable about proceeding.

Be prepared for questions such as:

How quickly do I have to change?
Can I go at my own pace?
Who is going to help me make the changes?
What support am I going to get?
What exactly is involved in each of these strategies?
Will I be negatively evaluated during the transitional period while I am experimenting?
What kind of resources are available to support me?
Do I have to do all this on my own time?

Don't be surprised if the questions are stated in a negative tone, since teachers will be feeling overwhelmed and uncertain about what is expected of them, and worried too, perhaps, that you think their previous practice has been unsatisfactory. Remember that change is a frightening process. Try to remain supportive when responding, recalling that the questions are not directed at you personally. Reinforce with your staff the idea that you are listening to their concerns, intend to address their questions, and will provide them with as much support as possible.

It is also important to be honest with them, letting them know, for example, what actual resources are available from the central office, especially if these are less than ideal, so that your staff can make realistic plans. In one school district, for example, a staff of thirty were given funds of $2,000 for their change project; they had to decide how the funds would be used to their best advantage. While the staff appreciated the amount that was given, they recognized that it was quite inadequate to effect extensive change in practice across the whole school. They decided, therefore, that the funds should be used for a few key staff members at each divisional level for the first year for such things as visits and conferences, and that the rest of the staff would donate their preparation time to cover for key staff members when they were away. The remaining funds were designated by staff for student learning materials.

Setting a School's Goals and Objectives Once your staff has determined the specific area of interest, develop a school goal statement and some action objectives. A sample goal statement is illustrated in Figure 4.4.

Figure 4.4

> # Our School Goal
>
> To involve our students in the writing process for the next year
> To meet this goal we will:
> Initiate daily writing
> Use student writing folders
> Promote diary writing
> Involve students in personal dictation
> Use conferencing strategies

This step also involves much discussion. Depending on the confidence of the staff, it may be decided that teachers need an overview workshop on process writing before they can develop realistic objectives.

Individual Goal Setting   Since individual teachers will have different strengths, needs, and learning styles, they may decide to develop their own goals and objectives within the global goal of the school. Some teachers, for example, prefer to read the theory and observe what others are doing before trying the strategies themselves. Others jump right in and try the strategies with children first and read about theory later. A few teachers may already feel comfortable with the school focus and may want to expand in another area of whole language. Support individual teachers in deciding on personal goals and objectives that suit them. It is not necessary that staff implement at the same speed or in the same manner. What is important is that they begin to grow.

Indicators for Growth   At the outset it is important to consider ways of monitoring teacher progress in implementing whole language. Growth can be evaluated both formatively (over time) and summatively (at the end of a given time period). Two instruments useful for indicating growth are the Whole Language School Assessment Inventory (see page 62) and the Whole Language Progress Indicator (see page 71). To determine how staff as a whole is progressing, invite them to use one of the instruments to rate themselves anonymously at the beginning of the year and again at the end of the year. Once the staff tallies the results they can determine the collective growth that has been made. The instruments can also be used by individual teachers over the course of a year to monitor their personal growth in implementing whole language. Or teachers can use the instruments at the end of specific time periods to evaluate personal progress.

Whole Language Resources   At this stage your teachers are going to want resources to start their implementation. There are four types of resources you will want to consider:

1. professional books on whole language that respond to theory and research
2. teacher resource books that put whole language into practice
3. materials for the classroom
4. whole language experts.

Before rushing out to purchase materials, make use of those you already have. Take an inventory by making a list of your listening centers, filmstrip machines, record players, listening tapes, videos, and films, and encourage teachers to use them in their classrooms. Invite the librarian to

Table 4.3
Whole Language Progress Indicator

Literature	*Grade* _____
Rate the items in the left-hand column below according to the numbers on the right:	1. once a day or more 2. twice weekly 3. weekly 4. twice monthly 5. monthly or less

Ideal image	*Classroom image*				
	1	*2*	*3*	*4*	*5*
quality literature is used					
teacher reads literature to the children					
students listen to literature at a listening center					
students have opportunities to read books of their choice					
thirty minutes is scheduled to read literature of students' choice					
students read fiction and nonfiction					
students are involved in shared reading					
students are involved in author studies (grades 2–8)					
students are involved in novel studies (grades 2–8)					
students are involved in drama and movement activities					

Comments:

Speaking	*Grade* _____

Ideal image	*Classroom image*				
	1	*2*	*3*	*4*	*5*
students discuss in whole class groups					
students discuss in groups of 5					
students discuss in groups of 2					
students participate in oral language center (role-play, puppet, drama, construction, etc.)					
students dictate chart stories					
students dictate personal stories (daily is impossible)					
students are involved in small group (5) problem-solving sessions					
students are involved in small groups (5) for communal tasks or projects					

Comments:

Writing	Grade _____

	Ideal image	Classroom image

Each student:		1	2	3	4	5
writes for 30 minutes or more						
writes in writing book						
uses writing folders (not for K-1)						
writes poetry						
writes information						
attends adult conference sessions						
participates in peer conferences						
responds to conferences						
generally revises once		yes				no
generally revises twice		yes				no
generally revises more than three times		yes				no
edits own work		yes				no
edits for peers		yes				no
publishes		yes				no

Comments:

Interpretive Activities	Grade _____

	Ideal image	Classroom image

	1	2	3	4	5
students participate in language centers					
students are assigned to centers					
students choose their centers					
students engage in one of these centers (listening, speaking, book corner, writing, creative art, drama, construction, modeling, research center)					
students participate in oral comprehension activities (discussions)					
students participate in written comprehension					

Comments:

Evaluation by the Teacher	*Grade* _____

Ideal image	*Classroom image*

	1	2	3	4	5
observes individual students as they read					
observes individual students as they write					
observes individual students as they engage in interpretive activities					
notes progress anecdotally					
records information on checklist and behavior inventories					
records information at small group discussions and conferences					
evaluates growth in language development over time					

Comments:

	Grade _____

Students' participation in non-*whole language activities*

	1	2	3	4	5
manipulated language basals					
handwriting lessons					
phonic lessons					
phonic worksheets					
spelling text exercises					
grammar worksheets					
basal reader workbooks					
skill workbooks					
skill-based language programs					

Teachers use:

	1	2	3	4	5
standardized tests to evaluate					
skill tests in words and grammar					
spelling tests					
basal reader levels as predominant evaluation strategy					

locate all the available pattern literature so that it can be used in shared reading and pattern writing. Find multiple copies of novels for group study. Consider making kits of numerous selections from a single author to start author units. Find out what resources other schools have that you can share, and investigate resources at the central office that can be borrowed. Publishing companies will often allow you to fieldtest materials for a reduction in price, so seek out their materials.

Invite your staff to develop a resource list of local teachers and consultants who might share their expertise with your staff when using whole language strategies, such as activity centers, shared reading, drama, dictation, theme units, novel studies, author studies, and process writing.

Gradually begin to add to your resources such items as big books, individualized novel kits, poetry books, literature kits, and some professional books on the "how to" of whole language. (A more complete listing starts on page 162.)

Implementation (1 to 2 Years)   The principal's role is crucial at this stage of the implementation process. You will need to obtain:

> financial commitment from superintendents for professional and student materials for the school
> professional development funds for conferences
> in-school supply teacher days for in-school and out-of-school visits
> in-service time from local consultants for classroom demonstrations and in-school workshops.

Implementation Plan   Consider setting up a small committee to use the data collected for developing an in-service plan for the year. The plan should be balanced between formal workshop presentations to in-class demonstrations by experts. It is also wise to schedule many sessions for discussion only, so that the staff can share some of their successes, as well as their concerns and questions. Provide in-school time for staff members to visit each others' classrooms to observe and learn from one another. In addition, provide time for the staff to visit other schools. Encourage teachers to choose a learning buddy on the staff or from another school with whom they can be really honest, and share their problems and frustrations. Watch for conferences that relate to your school focus and insure that some of your teachers attend. When key researchers are in town, make contact with them in advance and arrange for them to visit your school. If there are whole language support groups in your district, encourage your teachers to attend these, or start your own network.

Be sensitive to your teachers, give support as they indicate need, provide encouragement when they are frustrated, and celebrate with them when they share successes.

It is important that the implementation plan be flexible in order to accommodate for realistic implementation in the school. Very often staffs are overambitious in attempting to accomplish more than is reasonably possible. When this happens, change the plan (see Figure 4.5).

Figure 4.5

Implementation Plan		
Focus	Inservice	Date
Diary writing	˙Workshop by Reading consultant	Oct. 4
	· Staff coaches: Joel, Elain	Oct.- Jan.
	· Staff discussion	Oct.25
	· Staff discussion	Nov.20
Writing folders	· Workshop by Wayne	Dec. 3
	· Staff discussion	Dec. 15
	· Staff discussion	Jan.20
Conferencing	· Video on conferencing	Feb. 4
	·· Staff discussion	Feb .10
	·Classroom demonstration	Feb. 20
	· Coaching: Nick and Barb	Mar. 12
	· Staff discussion	Mar. 30

Problem-Solving   As implementation progresses, schedule frequent sessions where staff can react and share successes as well as failures. Identify the key obstacles and have the staff members themselves brainstorm for solutions, or call in consultants to share their solutions. Sometimes telephone an out-of-district expert to address a specific concern. When the staff realizes that you and their colleagues really care about overcoming the problems and will provide real support and encouragement, they are more willing to persevere in the implementation of whole language (see Figure 4.6).

Figure 4.6

Obstacles and Solutions	
Objective : To develop better conferencing skills	
Obstacles	Solutions
We don't know enough about the conferencing process.	· Invite a staff member to share ideas · Have an expert come to talk with the staff · Invite an expert to demonstrate conferencing in our classrooms · Read some books on conferencing · Try conferencing and share what worked.

Review for Continuation

Formative   On-going monitoring of growth in implementation can take place as the principal listens and makes suggestions during planned problem-solving sessions, during visits to classrooms, and during teacher-principal interaction sessions. Teachers can monitor their own growth as well by documenting changes they initiate in a personal log book. Many principals place a school log in the staff rooms in which teachers are encouraged to note the changes they are making. Documenting a journal article read, a center that was set up, or a shared reading session attempted is significant evidence that changes in beliefs and practices are happening. Encourage teachers to keep a personal diary of change behaviors as well (see Table 4.4).

Summative   One way to summatively evaluate progress in implementation is to invite the staff to complete the Whole Language Progress Indicator at the end of each year, and then invite a staff team to analyze and present the findings.

Implementation Process Time Line

As you can imagine, implementation takes time. It may take three to four years to complete all of the process (initiating the process, deciding which curricula to implement, school goals and action objectives, dealing with obstacles and problem-solving, and developing a school plan). But time is well spent because you will have involved the staff in their own process of change.

Summary

If the current impetus to whole language is to have a real impact on classroom practice we must consider a systematic, planned, teacher-focused implementation process. The plan in this book is a starting point presented with the hope that staffs will eventually develop their own individualized implementation process plan.

A process implementation model has many benefits:

trust within a school team develops
decision-making and power is in the teachers' hands, which gives them an incentive to grow actively
teachers' abilities and expertise are recognized and used productively through teacher-teacher coaching

teachers can prioritize a manageable number of changes in the curriculum so that they are not overburdened
continuity across the school is developed because everyone has the same priority
implementation truly becomes a process rather than an event
real growth in whole language occurs and is maintained.

ASSESSING PRINCIPAL'S EFFECTIVENESS IN IMPLEMENTING WHOLE LANGUAGE

Once your staff has begun to act on the school whole language implementation plan, you may periodically want to assess your effectiveness as a leader of whole language implementation. The checklist in Table 4.5 can be applied in different ways. You can use it yourself at different times during each year of the implementation plan in order to monitor your personal growth as an effective leader of schoolwide curriculum implementation. In addition, you may choose to have one or two trusted staff members use the instrument to assess your effectiveness. Some might invite the whole staff to use the checklist to give you on-going information about your role as implementation leader.

Table 4.4
Whole Language Implementation Log

Name of school: _____
(Who initiated: P (Principal), T (Teacher), C (Consultant), F (Outside facilitator)

Date	Who	Initiative	Comments
Oct. 5, 1986	P	Staff meeting to initiate school-based implementation process	Staff willing to be involved *Obstacles:* Staff felt overloaded; didn't have enough information
Jan. 9, 1987	F	Staff awareness of whole language (video).	Staff seems keen *Obstacles:* Whole language seems overwhelming; staff needs on-site support
Feb. 15, 1987	T	Read an article on writing process.	Have a little better understanding of the writing process *Obstacles:* How to find time
March 5	T	Tried daily writing in a writer's notebook	Kids seemed interested I didn't know how to extend the short stories they wrote.

Whole Language Implementation Log

Name of school: _____

(Who initiated: P (Principal), T (Teacher), C (Consultant), F (Outside facilitator)

Date	Who	Initiative	Comments (consequences, obstacles, suggestions to overcome obstacles, questions)

Table 4.5
Principal Checklist for Implementing Whole Language in a School

How effective is the principal in providing for:	*Ineffective*	*Somewhat effective*	*Effective*	*Very effective*
a school-based implementation process?				
an implementation plan?				
professional development for staff to become acquainted with whole language philosophy?				
professional reading material for teachers related to whole language?				
video, tape-slide, movies related to whole language?				
visits to other classrooms or schools where whole language has been implemented?				
support involvement, endorsement, and commitment of superintendents and trustees?				
central office resource staff?				
a variety of ways for staff in-service; *i.e.*, workshops, conferences, demonstrations, coaching?				
ways to communicate the whole language approach to parents?				
parent in-service about whole language?				
media awareness of quality learning occurring at the school?				
implementation profiles for growth in whole language?				
student profiles for growth in whole language?				
alternative whole language reporting procedures?				

5. Making the Transition from Traditional Approaches to Whole Language

Teachers make the transition to whole language in many different ways, depending largely on each teacher's learning style. Some hear about a new idea and jump right in and try it without initially giving much thought to the theoretical foundations, then later read the theory. Others read volumes of theory before they are willing to make a practical change. Many will follow advice from someone they respect—a colleague who has tried it, a local consultant who can demonstrate strategies for them, or a teacher from another school who has more experience with whole language. Some teachers like to make gradual incremental changes toward whole language, while others prefer to become totally immersed. Be prepared to support all these learning styles simultaneously. Provide "eager beavers" with immediate resources when they ask and at the same time be patient and accepting of those who ask questions, observe and read, but do not initially make any changes in teaching practices.

It is difficult to outline a consistent pattern of behavior that teachers demonstrate as they make the transition from traditional to whole language methods. In my experience most teachers experience a resistant stage. But when they begin to make actual changes in practice, the specific practice they choose to change, how they go about the change, and the speed of change varies from teacher to teacher.

I observed three of my colleagues make such changes as they developed whole language classrooms. Perhaps the experiences of Cathy Gregory, Wayne Gingrich, and Twila Brenneman will demonstrate how individual and complex the change process really is.

When I first met Cathy several years ago she ran an excellent traditional basal program for her first graders. The commercial readers reflected both phonetic and sight word philosophy. The vocabulary was learned through drills prior to reading texts, and the stories themselves repeated the vocabulary over and over. "Oh, look" and "see" tended to be the basic words in the early books, and the stories gradually extended from one or two phrases to several sentences by the end of the year. Cathy grouped her students according to reading ability, and each child progressed, at the group's pace, sequentially through the readers. Her students experienced a daily phonetic lesson, and completed a workbook or ditto page to reinforce the skill. Twice a week or so they all contributed sentences for a group chart based on some shared experience, and crayoned or painted a picture to match their dictated sentences. Writing stories consisted of filling in missing words or creating new pattern sentences based on a sentence given by the teacher. At the end of first grade most children could read the prescribed texts at grade level, could complete the workbook pages accurately, and could pass the required tests.

Naturally Cathy wasn't about to change a program that was so successful. When some new teachers came to the school she overheard numerous staff-room conversations about literature, shared reading strategies, the use of big books, and something called writing process. Although she rarely asked for professional assistance, I noticed that she began to listen in during meetings held between the other first grade teachers and the reading consultant. In the spring of that year Cathy signed up for a workshop on process writing and sat front row center.

During the fall of the second year she introduced journal writing to all her first graders and accepted developmental writing behaviors such as scribble, rhebus, random letters, and invented spellings. She was amazed at how quickly and how well the children began to write their own stories. In October of that year Cathy called her consultant and asked her to assess her low group because they couldn't read the words required in the first pre-primer. After involving this group of children in some shared reading strategies and dictated story activities the consultant discovered that all the children had the directionality skills of turning pages left to right and following text left to right across the page; they could recognize some words, such as "I," "to," and "and"; they could read in unison a story with a predictable pattern. The consultant recommended that Cathy drop the basal temporarily and do some shared reading activities and personal dictated stories with this group. In December Cathy noticed that her "low" group was now reading the basal better than the middle group, and so she began implementing shared reading and personal dictation with the rest of the class.

In her third year Cathy continued to use the traditional basal and maintained regular phonic lessons. However, she added shared reading strategies, weekly individual dictated stories, and process writing to her program.

During the fourth year she abandoned the traditional basal in favor of a literature-based commercial program, and continued to use Trade book literature, shared reading, and personal dictated stories. She realized that her students were learning phonetic skills within the writing process and through personal conferences, and so she finally gave up formal phonics lessons.

Wayne moved toward whole language based on intuition, experience, observation of students, and trust in his consultant. He had taught special education youngsters for years and had become disillusioned with the kinds of commercial programs available to them, programs with a strong phonetic orientation that didn't hold youngsters' interest. He had experimented with chart stories, and always read quality literature to the youngsters, but was frustrated because of the lack of variety and quality of student reading material. At first the consultant reinforced with him the whole language strategies in which he was already engaging his special education youngsters: group chart stories, literature readings, and activity centers. Then they discussed other whole language strategies he might try, such as sentence strip activities, weekly personal dictated stories, and shared reading strategies. Some commercial companies had recently published whole language literature-based reading programs, and so Wayne piloted some of the first materials. His school purchased sets of predictable pattern literature, and he combed the school and public libraries for additional predictable Trade book selections. The youngsters in his class began reading first in choral fashion, then elected to make big books of their own, brainstormed for new versions based on the same patterns, and gradually began to read the various selections with which they had worked. During the second year Wayne began publishing in class the students' dictated stories, and encouraged the children to write for themselves, accepting their emerging spelling and grammar skills. Wayne soon became a skilled practitioner, and began to read professionally to gain an understanding of the philosophical premises of whole language and insights for his own further growth.

Twila, an English as a Second Language (ESL) teacher, totally immersed her students in whole language after a few initial workshops she took. Traditional programs she had used were so irrelevant to her German-speaking Mennonite youngsters that she focused on personal dictated stories and writing process because the cultural experiences of her Mennonite children could be captured best in this way. The children told delightful stories, twenty or more sentences in length, of barn-raisings, quilting bees, shooting chicken hawks, and trapping raccoons. Twila recorded their individual stories each week in personal scrapbooks that they read to themselves and to each other. Some she published in cardboard covers and placed in the reading corner for others to read. The children wrote initially using pictures, scribble, and rhebus symbols, and gradually began to use invented and conventional spellings. She read specific literature that related to their Mennonite life to them, but also introduced Trade book literature that relates universally to all children. They enjoyed shared reading, making big books, and writing new pattern stories, and began to read and write with ease.

We have seen how three different teachers moved toward whole language programs, yet principals can play a key role in facilitating such growth. Developing an atmosphere of stimulation and support creates motivation and trust. At the same time principals need to recognize that change is slower in some than in others.

Give lots of initial resources for the quick starters and trust that the others will grow and learn at their pace, too. Locate consultant expertise if possible, but if your district doesn't have local language arts or reading consultants, then get in touch with publishing companies, universities, departments of education, or local TAWL groups for consultant expertise. Commercial programs that are literature-based and promote the writing process are also very useful for teachers who need day-to-day guidance in taking those initial steps toward whole language. You must be prudent, though, in the selection of such materials, because while many publishing companies claim to have whole language programs, many are incomplete. Get advice from a trusted expert.

As a general rule recommend that your teachers start small, and not change their whole program at once. Too much change too quickly makes teachers feel out of control, like a ship without a rudder, so that nothing seems to be progressing really well. I usually recommend starting with the writing process because the children make such visible and positive progress. In addition, there are fewer test score requirements associated with writing than in the area of reading.

Ideally a whole language classroom does not include a commercial basal program but uses only commercial Trade book literature. However, I feel it is unrealistic to expect teachers to make a quantum leap from a traditional skills-based basal to Trade book literature, and so I support the use of literature-based commercial programs as a transitional step toward a pure whole language program, providing teachers also develop individualized reading activities with quality Trade book literature. (See "Checklist for Basals," page 89.)

Table 5.1 illustrates a simplified profile through which teachers generally develop as they make the transition from traditional to a whole language classroom.

Table 5.1
Whole Language Implementation Phases

Typical Teacher Behaviors

Resistant phase
The teacher may:
demonstrate hostility to notions of change
defend existing programs
list numerous obstacles against whole language

Receptive phase
The teacher may:
begin to listen in on informal discussions about whole language
voluntarily come to networking sessions
begin to ask questions about whole language strategies
ask for professional material on whole language
ask for consultant assistance
request attendance at a conference on whole language
begin to attend a TAWL group

Experimental phase

The teacher may:
visit a classroom where whole language strategies are practiced
observe a specific whole language strategy
invite an expert to demonstrate a whole language strategy in the classroom
try one specific whole language strategy
share the positive and negative outcomes of the experience
begin to ask "what do you do when?" types of questions
come regularly to in-school networking sessions
share more positive than negative outcomes of whole language strategies
ask for specific materials required for the whole language strategy (*i.e.,* big books,
    writing folders)

Initiation phase

The teacher may:
give evidence in the classroom that a few whole language strategies are being used
    regularly (student-made big books are displayed; children work at a writing
    center; students listen at a listening center; students read individual literature
    selections; students engage in writing process)
continue to use many traditional strategies, such as phonic lessons, basal reader,
    and teacher-directed writing lessons
show enthusiasm for the whole language strategies they used
be willing to share with others the growth of their students
ask questions about specific whole language strategies he or she is using
ask questions about timetables and evaluation

Transitional phase

The teacher may:
begin to perfect the whole language strategies initiated
begin to add more whole language strategies to the program
begin to replace some traditional strategies with whole language strategies
show excitement for whole language results with students
continue to use some traditional strategies

Institutionalization phase

The teacher will:
begin to share willingly with other teachers how a whole language strategy is used
    with his or her students
begin to share personal adaptations and modifications of strategies used
use a predominance of whole language strategies
share strategies with teachers who are just beginning whole language
read professional articles, journals, and books
share favorite professional articles and books with others
receive visitors into the classroom to share a whole language strategy

Appendix

CHECKLIST FOR WHOLE LANGUAGE BASALS

Many commercial companies are developing what they call "whole language" reading programs, and some principals are purchasing class sets in the hope that these texts will do the job of implementing whole language in their schools. But be wary! Whole language has become the current educational "buzz" word, and everyone, including publishers, claims to have whole language programs. Examine commercial programs very carefully before you purchase them. Table 5.2 gives a checklist that may guide your decision.

Table 5.2
Checklist for Whole Language Basals

	Ineffective	Somewhat effective	Effective	Very effective
Literature				

How effective is this program in providing for:
   quality literature selections?
   unabridged literature selections?
   variety of literary genre (patterns, poetry, informational, fictional)?
   a variety of authors?
   biographies of authors?
   listings of high quality literature, supplemental selections?				

	Ineffective	Somewhat effective	Effective	Very effective
Integration				
How effective is this program in providing for:				
the integration of listening, speaking, reading, writing, drama, movement, and visual arts?				
thematic organization of stories and student activities?				
organizational strategies for the use of activity centers, such as book corners, listening post, drama center, construction area, art station, writing table?				
the integration of other content areas, such as mathematics, science, social studies, music, and physical education?				
Instructional Strategies				
How effective is this program in providing for:				
shared reading?				
book talks?				
choral speaking?				
story readings?				
storytelling?				
listening activities?				
co-operative learning?				
dramatization, such as role play, puppet plays, mime, improvization?				
debates?				
personal dictation?				
problem-solving activities?				
individualized reading?				
encouraging students to use a variety of reading strategies, such as pictures, pattern of the text,				

	Ineffective	Somewhat effective	Effective	Very effective
meaning, memory, context, and phonetics?				
student use of writing folders?				
student use of writing process (pre-writing, writing conferencing, drafting, revising, editing, publishing)?				
conferencing strategies?				
peer conferencing?				
experimentation with spelling, grammar, and usage?				
revising strategies?				
publishing strategies?				
Interpretive Activities for Students				
How effective is this program in providing for:				
interpretive activities, such as drama, role play, improvization movement?				
interpretive activities, such as discussions or debates?				
interpretive activities, such as painting, drawing, cut-and-paste, modeling, and construction?				
higher level thinking activities?				
comprehension activities?				
vocabulary study relative to the literature being read?				
a variety of reading strategies, such as close exercises, pattern awareness, meaning, memory, picture clues, and phonetics?				
phonetic activities that relate to reading and writing, oral as well as written?				
skill activities based on the needs of students?				

Evaluation	Ineffective	Somewhat effective	Effective	Very effective
How effective is this program in providing for:				
strategies for supporting teachers in observing students as they use language?				
varieties of formats for collecting information such as language samples, checklists, running records, etc.?				
opportunities for students to evaluate their language growth?				
samples of typical language behavior inventories?				
balance between standardized and informal evaluation procedures?				

6. Informing Parents about Whole Language

BUILDING PARENT SUPPORT FOR WHOLE LANGUAGE

The principal plays a key role in gaining parental support for whole language. Parents will count on both you and the teachers to explain the school's philosophy and to respond to their questions. Since whole language will be relatively new to many parents, it is important that you and your staff present a common philosophy, and that you share a commitment to that philosophy. It is not necessary for the principal to have the same in-depth knowledge of all the strategies of whole language that teachers will have in order to respond to parents, but you will feel more comfortable dealing with parent questions if you have a basic understanding of whole language philosophy. Get to know local principal, consultant, and teacher experts on whom you can call for additional support when you need it.

When and how to inform parents about your whole language program is an important consideration. Should you have an all-school curriculum night for parents and share the launching of your exciting new initiative with them, or do you take a more gradual approach? I prefer the second alternative for a number of reasons. Dealing with questions as they naturally arise from a few parents is easier than dealing with queries from fifty. Furthermore, in the initial stages of implementation you may not feel ready to respond to the concerns of large numbers of parents. So give yourself and your staff a chance to grow into whole language before engaging in a full-fledged parent in-service. After all, your responses are going to be more credible after you and your staff have had some real experiences with whole language and can cite some examples of growth of specific children in your school, rather than examples given in professional books.

It is also unfair to expect teachers to respond to parents before they have had a chance to implement some whole language strategies. Teachers need time to experiment, to overcome obstacles, to refine strategies, and to feel comfortable with what they are doing. So be patient. Give your staff resources, guidance, and support as they build confidence and expertise in various whole language strategies before you consider parent in-service. Once your teachers begin to share some successes with you and become more confident in using whole language, your staff may consider developing a plan for parental in-service that might include whole language information in newsletters, parent volunteer programs, classroom visits, coffee parties, or question-and-answer sessions.

Class Letters

Encourage individual teachers to send a classroom letter home to parents sharing examples of the growth of specific students in their classes. Include celebrations such as:

> Susan read one page of a big book all by herself.
> Harry dramatized a scene from *Charlotte's Web*.
> Paulo used phonetic spelling in his writing instead of scribble.
> Maria read a complete novel.
> Jasvinder revised his story three times before publishing it.

Teachers might even leave space in the letter for questions parents want to ask and that can be returned to the teacher for a future response.

School Newsletter

Keep in close communication with your teachers so that you become aware of parental questions as they emerge, and begin to place small items in the school newsletter to respond to these questions. Regularly include excerpts from professional articles to help parents build a basic understanding of whole language. Your local language arts consultant can suggest some pertinent articles to get you started, or use some of the information in this book. For example, the question-and-answer section (see page 37), the description of whole language strategies, or some comparisons between skills-based and whole language strategies (see page 13) may be useful. Also include success stories of children in your school. Celebrating the growth of individual children is one of the best ways to convince parents of the merit of whole language.

Literacy Stories

Invite your teachers to share with you special literacy events in their classrooms, and have them write a small article for parents and staff to enjoy. Here is a sample from the Sandowne School located in Waterloo, Ontario, Canada:

Writing at Sandowne

Teachers are excited about writing instruction in our classrooms at Sandowne School and we are learning from the children as well. Periodically, we will be sharing a literacy story with you so that you too can experience the joy we are feeling.

Literacy Story about Matthew Stuart

Grade One

(Written by Gail Heald-Taylor)

Matthew Stuart marched confidently from his first grade classroom into my office, his story about his grandma tucked under his arm. "Want to hear my story Mrs. Heald-Taylor?" he announced. "Sure," I said, as I put down the duty schedule I was working on so I could give him my undivided attention. "Let's sit down together so you can read it to me."

With pride he placed his book between us, opened the orange cover and enthusiastically began to read, moving his little finger left to right across the page, pausing slightly at each individual word. My eyes followed across the lines of print, page by page to the end of the story.

" I DUG A HOWL FOR GRAMA
ANd I POUT GRAMdA IN IT
A NO I TiKLD HR TOO.
I WONTid TO SHO GRAMdA
HAW I KOd skoobA.

div

I built A SAnd CASTL BUT A
BIG WAvE CAmE.
GRAMA SAd THET'S WUT HAPiuG
TO SANd CASLS ANd WE wiL
BiLb A NUTHR ONE NEKS TIM
I BOT HOT DOGS FOR mE ANd
GRAMA BUT THA FEL IN tHE
SANd so I HAd TO WoSH
THEM ofF. "

When he had finished reading he looked up at me with a big grin. "Matthew," I marvelled, "your story makes me feel like I'm on the beach too. I can just feel the hot sand, hear the wind and the sound of your grandma laughing as you covered her with sand and tickled her toes. And I'm also really impressed with how well you read your story."

"I know," he replied eagerly, "now you read it."

"Oh no," I thought, "what if I make a mistake?" Even though I've had lots of practice reading stories with invented spellings, I'm always afraid that it will be embarrassing to the author if I don't read it with ease. "Will you help me if I need it," I asked.

"You bet," he replied. "I help Mrs. Braun all the time."

And so I began with Matthew guiding me.

I dug a hole for grandma
and I put grandma in it,
and I tickled her toe.
I wanted to show grandma
how I could scuba
dive.
I built a sand castle but a
big wave came.
Grandma said, "That's what happens
to sand castles and we will
build another one next time.
I bought hot dogs for me and
grandma but they fell in the
sand, so I had to wash
them off.

As I read I was amazed at all the language Matthew had mastered. He obviously understood the story *Just Grandma and Me* by Mercer Mayer that Mrs. Braun had read to the children, but then he was able to write his own version based on the book. His story provided for the reader numerous sensory images of the beach: 'Grandma covered with sand, except for her toes; a child pretending to scuba dive; a sand castle being washed away by a wave. . . .' And just as real authors do, Matthew had managed to convey the loving, happy, playful relationship he has with his own grandma. Then I noticed all the conventions of writing he used. He left spaces between words; he put periods at the end of the lines; he spelled 21 words completely:

(I, dug, a, for, and, to, built, but, it,
big, wave, came, sand, we, one, hot,
dogs, me, in, them, off);

he used phonetic strategies to spell most of the others:

(wontid for wanted ; skooba for scuba ;
castl for castle; thet's for that's)

I also noticed how he experimented with contractions: thet's for that's, and how close his approximation actually was! He even self-corrected his work when he changed LIKLD to TIKLD, probably after he re-read his piece and realized that he wanted the word tickled rather than liked.

Interrupting my thoughts, Matthew put learning back into perspective. "Boy," he remarked, "you did really good. You know, when Mrs. Braun read my story today she didn't need any help from me at all. She's *really* getting to be a good reader!"

We parents can learn a great deal from Matthew's writing. Initially, his classroom writing experiences are quite different from writing lessons in classrooms twenty or thirty years ago. When we were in first grade, writing time was taken up with hand writing exercises, phonic lessons or copying from the blackboard poems or sentences initiated by the teacher. Composing a complete story about a personal experience was usually reserved for students in later grades when they were ready.

Matthew, on the other hand, was provided invitations to write even before he entered grade one and has written stories all year long. He believes in himself as a reader and writer knowing he can compose real stories; that he can spell many words; that he can use phonetic strategies to spell others; and that he can assist adults in the reading process as well! Naturally, he has not mastered *all* there is to know about writing conventions; after all he *is* only in grade one.

Work Samples

Students love signing out class big books or student-published books (second editions only) to take home. Encourage teachers to add blank pages to the books and invite parents to make comments. On parent nights teachers can display writing samples to show a range of progress that students themselves have selected to share.

Mini-Celebration

Communicating frequently with students' homes, by sending "Good

Work" certificates, notes, or through telephone calls is an excellent strategy to promote whole language. Have teachers encourage students to write the notes and make the phone calls themselves so as to share a personal success story with Mom and Dad.

Classroom In-service

Some teachers may want to respond to parents before others do so. Give your first risk-taker plenty of support. Make the local language arts consultant available, provide overheads if needed, print professional articles or handouts, and *you* provide the cookies and coffee. Allow the teacher to choose the format of the in-service that suits him or her. Perhaps it will be a series of small-group visits to the classroom, a discussion over coffee (you provide the supply teacher), or an evening session. Encourage teachers to keep the in-service informal, providing lots of opportunities for questions and discussion. Have teachers record the questions, if possible, so that further information or in-service can be provided for parents later.

Teacher-Student Parent Night

Encourage individual teachers to do in-service with their students at each activity center concerning what is learned in the whole language classroom. These subjects would include what they do at literature sharing time and how they go about writing. Then have students take their parents around the room and respond to any questions. Have a general session at the end of the evening where teachers can respond to any question the parents have. Some whole language teachers invite parents to participate in whole language activities so as to demonstrate to them that learning has taken place despite the absence of worksheets.

Parent Volunteers

When your staff begins to share successes with you and indicates a sense of comfort with one or two whole language strategies, you may consider setting up a volunteer program. Start with a small group at first and provide them with some initial in-service. You or your local consultant could discuss whole language philosophy with them, and then take them to a few classrooms to see whole language in action. Spend a great deal of time with this nucleus of parents to answer questions and to outline ways they can support whole language strategies as volunteers. Support teachers in responding to parent volunteer questions as they arise, and plan frequent opportunities for volunteer get-togethers for informal discussions about whole language philosophy, strategies, and specific problems. Once these parents become convinced of the merit of whole language they will build whole language support in the community. These parents can also be involved in planning future parent in-service.

Question-and-Answer Sessions

When parents across the school begin to ask questions about whole language you may schedule small informal question-and-answer sessions with groups of parents. They will probably want to know how phonics will be taught, how teachers deal with spelling, how standards will be maintained. Responses to the usual questions are given in the question-and-answer section of this book. Don't feel you have to answer all the questions alone; bring along a capable teacher to assist or a local consultant for support.

Media Presentation

Near the end of your first year of implementation prepare a video or tape-slide presentation of your school showing an overview of whole language. Parents who see their children actively engaged in language learning on screen make a powerful support for whole language. There are many commercial tapes available as well that can give parents an overview of whole language. Heinneman Publishers; Holt, Rinehart and Winston, Canada; and Richard C. Owen Publishers have some excellent audiovisual materials that you can purchase.

School Curriculum Night

When you are in your second year of implementation, consider inviting parents into the school for a curriculum in-service night where you share with them the whole language goals of the school, the media presentation, and the applications of whole language at particular grade levels discussed by individual teachers. Equip your staff with some prepared overheads, *i.e.*, the principles of whole language (see page 15) or the whole language strategy overview (see page 20), and any other relevant material from this book that will support your teachers. Encourage teachers to demonstrate some whole language success stories through their students' work.

Letters to Celebrate Success

Periodically it is a good idea for teachers to take a class inventory of all the strategies students are using and send a note home to parents sharing this knowledge. Here is an example:

Grade Six
Sandowne School

Dear Parents,

I have been very excited about the growth the students have made in language arts this year. I am especially pleased with what they have learned in the area of writing. Last week they shared with me what they knew, and I was overwhelmed with their responses. I thought that you might be interested and so I will list their ideas.

What your children know about writing:

how to choose topics
how to get ideas
how to write drafts
drafts are usually messy
how to interview
how to write long stories
to write what you know a lot about
how to write believable stories
experimenting with different story structures

experimenting with different genre
how to share writing strategies in stories
how to conference with a friend
how to ask the group for suggestions
how to write interesting leads
how to give positive responses
how to work in groups
how to give positive suggestions
how to redraft
strategies for adding information (arrows, cut and paste, redrafting)
how to revise to make the story more interesting, clearer, more descriptive for
   the reader
to be aware of the audience
how to add more detail, information
how to describe characters, setting, action
how to build a problem into stories
how to build suspense
how to show feelings in stories
how to build a character
how to create action
sharing thoughts of characters
writing from different points of view
developing voice in the story
how to use figures of speech, such as metaphors, similes, personification
how to use dialogue
mechanics, such as using capitals, punctuation, contractions, possessives, plu-
   rals, tenses, compound words, adjectives, complete sentences
spelling strategies, such as visual awareness, phonetics, editing, dictionary use,
   writing
how to edit and proofread
how to end stories
when to abandon stories
how to delete parts

While this list is a compilation of the whole class, not every child will have experimented with every strategy. I do want to stress, however, that most of the class has attempted most of the strategies listed.

I am delighted with their progress as I am sure you are. Please discuss this list with your children and have them share with you the strategies they know in one of their favorite selections.

Please write or call if you have any questions.

Dear Parents:

I am amazed at how much the students have learned about writing this year. In the fall term only one or two students took the risk to revise parts of a story they had written. Shawn was one of the first when he added some beautiful descriptive language to the scene of him fishing on the lake.

By the winter term, most students became aware of various writing strategies real authors use in literature and they too began to incorporate these strategies into their own pieces. Mike moved from fantasy stories to realistic fiction and made his "Party" story seem very real. Emma realized that her "Cousin" story had become monotonous in parts and in revising it for publication chopped the boring parts out. She also worked out a moral issue of "stealing" very believably through the actions, dialogue, and thoughts of her characters. Brian's "Hiking" story was loaded with suspense when one of his friends fell through the ice. He added a lot of intricate detail to his story so that the audience (readers) could imagine that they too were dangling in the freezing water. Sandy's story about "Chad" had wide appeal to sixth graders because she held us all in suspense wondering if the boy and girl in the story were going to go to the dance together, and of course become friends. Sandy's story stimulated many stories based on a similar theme. Jane is working on a story where the main character is sneaking out to go to a school dance, but feels very guilty leaving her young brother with a babysitter she has hired with her pocket money, even though *she* was supposed to have been in charge of his care.

This term has been phenomenal for writing growth. It has been fascinating observing how individual writers go about the process of writing. Heather says that for her the story, poem, or melodrama just "comes out" when she puts pencil to paper. She says she doesn't know what she's going to say, or what genre she'll use beforehand. Jenni, on the other hand, says that she pre-plans parts of her stories and then tests her ideas out orally with her friends, in conference sessions, and with her parents to be sure the situations and dialogue are believable *before* she writes. At one point I got really frustrated because for more than a week nothing had gotten written in her "Amanda" story, even though she had discussed her solutions to the problem in her story in our group share session, with me at lunchtime, with a friend while she was on phone check, and even went home with a friend for lunch one day to check out with her friend's parent the plausibility of an action of one of her characters. Finally, I told her, "Jenni, just get some ideas down on paper, you can revise them later."

Another week passed before pencil moved on the paper. But when she got going she completed that section in a couple of days; the actions of her character were believable, the dialogue was realistic, and the emotions of the character were true to life!

Many youngsters are experimenting with, and are successfully using dialogue; Craig Hunter, Drew, Michelle, Linda, Becky, Jason, Mark, and Lisa are doing a fine job of this.

Students are also writing varieties of genre: Kim's story of when she ran away as a little girl is somewhat autobiographical; Craig Cardiff, Matt, Heather, Craig Hunter, and Erik have experimented with poetry; David, Drew, Jonathan, Jason, and Justin enjoy writing adventure stories; Janet and Heather have written mysteries; Melissa, Emma, Michelle, Linda, Andrea, and Jonathan have written narratives of real experiences; most students have written realistic fiction, fantasy, research reports, and letters.

Ending stories has been difficult for many students. Some rely on time as a guide: and then we went home; and then we got an award; and then I woke up from the dream; and then I got away from . . . Justin got so frustrated with how to end one of his stories that he decided to have all the characters die!

Most of our young writers are creating realistic scenes for their stories. Shawn redrafted the opening paragraph of one of his stories three times before he felt comfortable with his setting. Janet described the walk in the forest with such detail that her readers felt they were there. Barbara's story of the lost lamb came to life through her description of the craggy rocks and the bleating of the wooly lamb.

I have encouraged the class to become aware of experiences around them on a day-to-day basis that could become a story, and to jot down visual impressions, smells, sounds, and feelings they remember. Kim first experimented with these vignettes of life when she was in Florida this spring and wrote the story about "Life as a Newspaper," "The Heron's Trick," and "Life in Gate 13."

Then one morning Melissa danced into the classroom with her beach hat cocked to one side and announced to everyone that she'd seen this funny old man on the bus that morning and she just had to write about it. Here is her beginning . . .

> It was a cold and wet Thursday. The sky was like a thick gray blanket that seemed to cover the world. A light drizzle was falling and the street was sleek from being wet. I was waiting for the bus. My fingers were numb from the cold, and my shoes were soaked. The bus slowly turned the corner.
>
> "Finally," I muttered as the bus stopped. It was crowded but it seemed to have a warm feeling. I wasn't sure where I wanted to sit . . . but then I saw him.

Not only have the children learned composing strategies but they have also learned skills of spelling, mechanics, and grammar as well. Although we rarely have formal whole class lessons, the children have naturally learned these skills. First of all the children became aware of spelling, mechanics, and grammar as they read quality literature selections all year long. When they turn in their writing folders and I respond to their stories, I note for them the writing skills they are using appropriately and also point out areas they should work on (*i.e.*, possessives, use of periods or quotation marks). In addition, I note incomplete spelling and encourage the children to complete these spellings when they edit their pieces for publication. On an on-going basis I refer to a grammar scope and sequence chart at the sixth grade level in a current commercial program. I often find that our students know the designated requirements plus many additional skills.

I do appreciate your support this year, and it has played a major role in your child's growth. You encouraged your children as they gradually gained faith in themselves as learners and delighted in their accomplishments as writers and readers. For many children the development has been phenomenal; for a few it was a year of planting seeds for new ways of learning. These seeds have germinated and begun to sprout. In time, if nurtured, they will grow and bloom. This has been a significant year for this sixth-grade class. They have experienced rich literature and have participated in the writing process just as real authors do. For many, they will truly become lifelong readers and writers.

It has been a real honor working with your children this year. We have shared so much together.

Next year I will be teaching at the University of Windsor at the Faculty of Education and I would like to share your children's literacy development with the student teachers to show them how exciting and rewarding integrated student centered learning can really be.

I will miss my class in P. 2. at Sandowne School, but memories of this year will be captured as I read and share their stories and as I write about my experiences with them.

WHOLE LANGUAGE TIPS FOR PARENTS

Most parents want to support their youngsters at home and may request specific ideas for doing so. Here are some general activities that are appropriate for students from kindergarten to sixth grade that your teachers could duplicate and provide for the parents at an in-service session or during parent interviews. The ideas are written with the parents as the audience, so that they can be duplicated as given here.

Photo Album

As pictures are taken and placed in an album have the children dictate a lengthy story to go with each photograph while you write it down for them. Continue to print the dictated story for your older youngsters as well, even though they may be able to write for themselves. In this way they are developing oral language skills, as well as composing ability. Read the story back to the young children, and listen while your older children read their own. Make duplicate photos that can be bound into a special birthday book or Christmas present for grandparents.

Scrapbook

After a trip to an aquarium, science center or local fair have the children make crayon pictures of the events that impressed them and record oral stories (five to ten sentences) to go with each illustration.

Birthday Book

On each birthday give a child a birthday book and label it "When I Was Five," "When I Was Eleven." Encourage the child to paste important cards, ticket stubs, postcards, awards in the book. Invite the child to dictate or write stories to accompany some of the entries.

Gift Book

A wonderful present for Mom, Dad, or Grandparents is to make a cloth-covered book of family pictures and stories. "Grandma and Me," "Grandma and Me at the Park," "Last Summer at the Cottage" are possible titles.

Trip Book

Children can dictate or write a travelogue to highlight the key events of an excursion or trip. Attach related photos, postcards, brochures, and pamphlets.

Diary

Purchase blank-page books for the children so that they can write about events that are important to them. Encourage pre-school children to keep a diary. Initially, younger children may dictate happenings so that you can print these into their books, but they can draw their own pictures as well as communicate their stories through scribble and invented letters. Older children may make entries that are both public and private. Respect their rights and *don't* read entries unless the child gives you permission.

Messages

Send fun messages to your children in their lunch boxes, under their pillows, or under a pile of dirty clothes not yet put in the laundry. And encourage a response. Some parents have reported that these written conversations can go on for days.

Written Conversations

Written conversations are a wonderful whole language strategy to use when you and your child are having a disagreement. For example, if your child has neglected to take the garbage out three out of seven days of the week and you're really angry about it, sit down with your child and, rather than shouting at him or her, try writing down how you feel and then have the child respond—in writing. Somehow the act of writing it down appears to diffuse the anger and at the same time forces your youngster to respond rather than "turning you off," as so often happens when we berate someone.

Family History

Should you have an elderly parent, grandparent, aunt, or uncle, invite your child to interview that person and record the stories on a tape recorder. Then transcribe favorite stories and make a family book of "Great Uncle Louis" by including photographs as well as text.

Read to Your Children

Read favorite stories to your children even when they can read for themselves. Children of all ages enjoy family story readings, especially if the entire story is read. This is preferable to engaging them in reading a portion of the text. Children get very anxious when they have to perform for you in round-robin-reading fashion, knowing that you are probably evaluating their reading skills as they go through their portion. So make story reading time a pure act of joy, trusting that sharing favorite stories with your children is the best way to cultivate a love of literature.

Tell Stories to Your Children

Dig out some of your old photograph albums when you were young, and tell your children about the "good old days." Consider re-organizing some of the albums and attach lengthy dictated or written vignettes to go with clusters of pictures.

Take Children on Excursions

Whenever you go shopping, to the garage, or for a haircut take your children with you and respond to their questions, or allow them to ask the expert what they want to know. Special excursions are also valuable in extending your child's knowledge; for example, going to the park, to a local festival, to a parade, a museum, an art gallery, or going camping.

7. Assessing Student Growth

STUDENT EVALUATION

The key issue of whole language evaluation is in direct conflict with traditional evaluation methods, and therefore both teachers and parents will want to be assured that language progress can be effectively evaluated and that standards will be maintained. This is your goal as principal as well, so you will need to have available alternative evaluation procedures that are consistent with whole language philosophy, and be able to justify their use to your teachers and to the community. The first task you will face is convincing teachers and parents that traditionally used standardized tests are no longer relevant: Standardized tests are not congruent with new research in language training; they are skill, not process, oriented; they are used to sort and classify youngsters rather than to give direction for learning; they are incomplete; and they have a mistaken aura of objectivity. In schools across the United States it is almost blasphemous to question the use of standardized tests because they are so institutionalized at school district, state, and federal levels. So your task is not an easy one.

A strategy I have found useful in my fight against standardized tests is to cite what research says about their use. Then standardized test supporters can't accuse you of being opinionated; you're merely sharing the views of current researchers. To provide you with a defensible stand, I have prepared the following (over-referenced) response that you may duplicate for your staff or for parents.

The Perils of Standardized Tests

Standardized tests have remained the same for virtually fifty years and have not kept pace with current research in language development (Pearson, 1985; Valencia and Pearson, 1987; Farr and Carey, 1986; Pearson and Dunning, 1985). Standardized tests, for example, reflect the behavioral research of thirty years ago, and are based on the assumption that language is taught through direct instruction of isolated skills hierarchically organized and mastered one level at a time (Valencia and Pearson). Whole language, on the other hand, is based on current research that supports the notion that language is learned through a thinking, social, participatory, interactive process as youngsters engage in rich literate experiences (listening, speaking, reading, and writing) right from birth (Chomsky, 1972; Clay, 1975, 1977; Doake, 1980; Goodman, K., 1972, 1974, 1977; Goodman, Y., 1980; Graves, 1978, 1982, 1984; Harste, 1984; Holdaway, 1979; Smith, 1971, 1983). Therefore, process knowledge, as well as skills knowledge, is important in whole language assessment (Collins, Brown and Larkin, 1980; Pearson and Spiro, 1980; Spiro and Meyers, 1984; Teale, Hiebert and Chittenden, 1987; Wittrock, 1987).

Purposes for evaluation also differ. In skills-based evaluation standardized test results are used for promoting students; selecting youngsters for enrichment or remediation; comparing student to student, school to school, state to state, and, in some instances, to evaluate effective schools and teachers (Fisher *et al.,* 1978; Johnston, 1987). While these tests were not designed to make program recommendations conscientious teachers look to tests as guides for instruction (Valencia and Pearson), and run the risk that the standardized test is the tail that wags the instructional dog (Darling-Hammond and Wise, 1985; Durkin, 1987; Popham, 1985; Shannon, 1986), keeping instructional practice in an outdated time warp. So entrenched are standardized tests in North America that new programs based on current research are often abandoned based on test score results (Valencia and Pearson). Thus standardized tests contribute to the maintenance of the status quo in classroom practice. While the goal of standardized tests is for classification, accountability, and progress monitoring (Johnston), evaluation in the whole language approach provides optimal instruction for all students. Instruction-linked evaluation as assessment is the gathering of information to meet the diverse needs of individual students (Teale *et al.*, 1987).

One way assessment can be linked to instruction is for teachers to interact with students as they engage in the act of reading and writing, intervening to provide support or make suggestions when students appear to have difficulty (Campione and Brown, 1985). Therefore, assessment in whole language classrooms is conducted to identify strategies and behaviors in which youngsters engage as their language grows and develops, so that teachers can initiate instructional situations to promote continuous growth.

Standardized tests are also inappropriate for whole language because they are an incomplete measure of language learning, since they mainly address reading and ignore other important components of the language arts such as listening, speaking, and written expression which are so valued in the whole language approach. Standardized reading tests are problematic since they evaluate only a narrow range of the knowledge and skills involved in reading (Baker and Herman, 1985). Primary reading tests, for example, usually focus on phonetic knowledge and vocabulary recognition, largely ignoring other very important aspects of the reading process such as background knowledge, directionality, meaning-seeking strategies, print awareness, tracking ability, understanding of characters and events in stories, appreciation of authors, and interest in reading. Standardized tests also assume the youngster has already begun to read, and therefore fail to measure language behavior in the early stages of reading—such as page turning, talking like a book, finger pointing, and picture reading (Teale *et al.*) Standardized reading tests focus mainly on abstract concepts of the reading process, such as phonetics, before youngsters are developmentally ready for such understanding.

Valencia and Pearson cite two other dangers associated with standardized tests: One lies in the false sense of security when we equate skilled reading with scores on our current reading tests; another stems from the aura of objectivity associated with published tests, and the corollary taint of subjectivity associated with informal assessment. Sometimes data from standardized tests are thought by teachers, principals, and administrators to be more trustworthy than daily data collected through observation. Johnston maintains that observational evaluation *is* the real evaluation that should form the basis for instructional decisions far more than formal test scores (Shavelson and Stern, 1981).

If standardized tests are inappropriate for evaluating language growth, what alternative evaluation strategies can be used? More accurate and significant information regarding a student's growth in language can be obtained by observing what youngsters do as they are engaged in the language process (Valencia and Pearson; Wittrock, 1987; Johnston; Teale *et al.*). What do youngsters do, for example, when they are reading? Is the "reading" a retold approximation or accurate reconstruction of the text? Does the student point to words and attempt to make an oral match? Does the student try to get meaning from the text? What strategies does the student use to get meaning from print? Does the student read unfamiliar books as well as rehearsed selections? Does the student choose to read and have favorite genre and authors? The answers to these questions give teachers real data about each student's language ability as well as insights regarding possible program options. These data obtained through teacher observations provide a broader amount and richer quality of information about the reading process than do standardized tests (Ruth, 1987; Teale *et al.*; Valencia and Pearson; Wittrock).

But teachers need support in developing expertise in observation strategies: in knowing how and what to observe, developing varieties of formats to collect information, and understanding the significance of the data for instructional programming.

Whole Language Observation

Observing youngsters as they engage in using language is the key strategy in whole language evaluation. The actual behavior that youngsters demonstrate in the process of listening, speaking, reading, and writing are beginning to emerge in the research literature (Applebee, 1980; Clay, 1979; Genishi and Dyson, 1984; Goodman, Y., 1981; Heald-Taylor, 1985, 1986; Jensen, 1984; Sulzby, 1983, 1985; Sulzby and Teale, 1985;

Teale and Sulzby, 1986). The "Whole Language Behavior Inventory" (see page 128) has identified some of these behaviors in language areas (listening, speaking, reading, and writing) for youngsters in the kindergarten to sixth grades that will serve as a developmental guide for teachers. Assessment information can also be collected about language learning on anecdotal records, checklists, log books, attitude inventories, and language behavior inventories, to name only a few (Teale *et al.*). Teachers are encouraged to use a variety of formats to collect as much information as possible about a student's development and in as many different contexts. Researchers claim that trained teachers in whole language philosophy are the best interpreters of data (Clay; Johnston; Ruth; Teale *et al.*) to be used for making judgments regarding program strategies, in reporting to parents, and in making decisions for grade placement. There is no substitute for an informed, knowledgeable professional teacher for making such evaluative decisions.

Data Collection Formats

A variety of samples of data collection formats useful in whole language philosophy for students in kindergarten to sixth grade are described below. Five main formats are used:

1. anecdotal records
2. log books
3. checklists
4. inventories
5. work samples.

Student behaviors are listed on some formats but these characteristics are not in any absolute order, since students develop in very individual ways.

Anecdotal Records

Anecdotal records can be kept for students in kindergarten to sixth grade in any of the language areas. Note some of the key behaviors at the top of the anecdotal record sheet, and record what you notice as you observe children engaged in various activities (see Figure 7.1). Attach the anecdotal sheet to your clipboard as you work with the children.

Listening				
enjoys listening to stories listens to peers in conversations listens for information listens to peers in group activities Comprehends what is heard			
Al	**Elizabeth**	**Gary**	**Jill**
appears attentive, but doesn't follow directions	listens to and recalls details	can retell stories that have been read to him	listens thoughtfully to others' ideas

Log Books

Log books are small folders kept by each student to document language growth. Both students and teachers can record information (see Figure 7.2).

Figure 7.2
Example of a Log Book

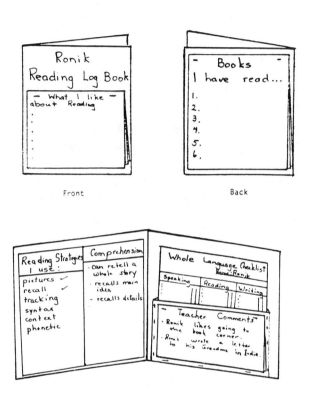

Front   Back

Inside

Writing Log

The writing log, which is stored in each student's writing folder, is an excellent way to keep on-going records of student writing progress. Teachers divide an 8½″ × 11″ paper into four columns:

1. response to draft
2. strategies I use well
3. strategies I am working on
4. spelling I need to edit

As the teacher reads a draft of a particular story he or she documents information for students so that they become aware of this data for personal growth. Eventually, strategies from column three move to column two, when students gain proficiency in an area. This information is also valuable for reporting student progress to parents (see Figure 7.3).

Figure 7.3

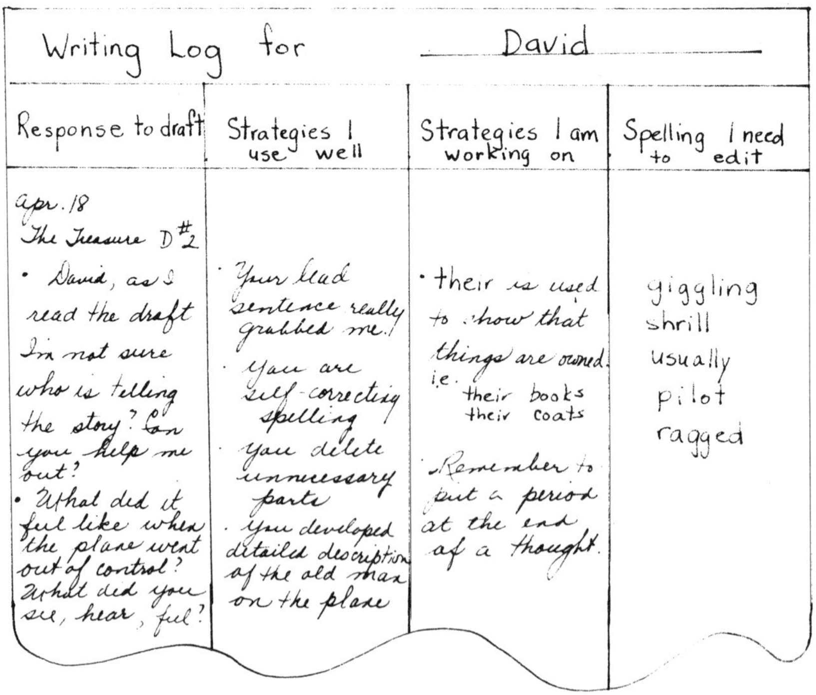

Writing Log for David

Response to draft	Strategies I use well	Strategies I am working on	Spelling I need to edit
apr. 18 The Treasure D #2 • David, as I read the draft I'm not sure who is telling the story? Can you help me out? • What did it feel like when the plane went out of control? What did you see, hear, feel?	· Your lead sentence really grabbed me. · You are self-correcting spelling · You delete unnecessary parts · You developed detailed description of the old man on the plane	· their is used to show that things are owned. i.e. their books their coats · Remember to put a period at the end of a thought.	giggling shrill usually pilot ragged

Checklists

Checklists can be developed that are not as demanding on teachers' time as anecdotal comments. Develop a format that is easy for teachers to use in recording growth that includes typical behavior from the "Whole Language Behavior Inventory" (see Table 7.1).

Table 7.1
Spelling: Inventory (Wendy Simpson and Gail Snider)

S = Sept.	Scribble	Consonant spelling	Invented spelling	Transitional spelling invented→correct	Comments
O = Oct. N = Nov. D = Dec. Ja = Jan. F = Feb. M = March Ma = May Ju = June Name Date	Story scribble / Sentence scribble / Word scribble / Random letters	Initial consonants / Final consonants / Familiar words / Integration (words, letters, scribble) / Number of sentences	Consonant spelling / Vowels in spelling / Transition to correct spelling	¾ invented spelling / ½ invented spelling / Number of sentences / ⅔ correct spelling / ¾ correct spelling / Uses periods / Uses capitals / Number of sentences	
Tony Mary	S S O O	N			

Running Record

A running record in the reading process is a useful way to determine the type of miscues (verbal substitutions in reading) youngsters make while reading a particular text. Running records give teachers insight into a child's word knowledge, reading strategies used, and comprehension. Students are given text at their developmental level and are asked to read it orally. As the student reads, the teacher marks a duplicate copy of the text to indicate these points:

accurate reading (✔)

substitutions (home / house)

repeating or rereading (Little brown mouse)

omission (Little Brown Mouse)

an insertion (Little Brown Mouse saw a pretty red flower)

self-correction (Little Brown Mouse saw a was(sk) black beetle).

By comparing the error rate to the number of words read, the teacher can determine whether the text is too difficult, the kinds of strategies the student uses (phonetics, meaning, rereading), and the vocabulary knowledge of the student.

Work Samples

Samples of work over time are one of the best ways to show growth in language development. Tapes of children's storytelling and dictated stories over time are good ways to show improvement in oral language development and quality of composition. Writing samples over time provide real evidence of growth in handwriting, spelling, conventions of punctuation and grammar, and composition.

In Michael's four writing samples (see Figure 7.4), for example, his use of symbols to record stories developed from scribble, invented letters, upper-case conventional letters to conventional use of upper and lower case. Spelling stages evident in his writing are pre-phonemic (no sound-symbol correspondence); visual spelling (words he recognizes in reading such as spook, ghost, and his name); phonetic spelling (waz for was, vairy for very), and finally conventional spelling. In the fall he spelled two words conventionally, in the winter forty-three, and eighty-four conventional

Figure 7.4
Michael's Writing
Age 6—September to June

Michael Age 6.   December

I got two ᵓCyclopedias.
and I got one chocolate
bunny. I got 36 eggs.
David waz running on
he hert his foot.
are baby brother got
the most eggs he had
ᵓᵃ. an David got
46 eggs.
Michael Age 6. March

The big goast

One day a big goast came. I got vairy skaird I ran aroan but the goast sot up to me. every time I ran right in my house. My mom told me to go owtside But but what f thair is a goast owtside. oh oh rily, a goast But thair is a goast owtside you go owtside you will see a goast. I wil but I wil not see a goast. So my mom went owtside. I saw a goast but it wil go alway at night and it did. and never came back.

Michael Age 6. May

spellings in the spring. Michael also gained knowledge of print conventions over the course of the year. In September his text (scribble) moves left to right across the pages, while in December spaces emerge between words (and between the scribble for intended words). By March he had begun to use some punctuation, and in June he was generally using capitals appropriately. His composing ability grew as well. His Christmas letter is a chaining of ideas; in March he wrote a narrative; and by May he invented a fantasy story that had several ideas about one topic. In his May story he used many techniques of real authors, such as a story problem, suspense, and resolution.

Self Evaluation

Students of all ages enjoy being involved in sharing what they think they know. Often, however, we educators fail to ask them. Younger students might be asked questions orally, and symbols to circle can be given to them (see Figure 7.5).

Figure 7.5
Reading Attitude Inventory

---

1. How do you feel when your teacher reads a story aloud?

2. How do you feel when someone gives you a book for a present?

3. How do you feel about reading books for fun at home?

4. How do you feel when you are asked to read aloud to your group?

5. How do you feel when you are asked to read aloud to your teacher?

6. How do you feel when you come to a word you don't know?

7. How do you feel when it is time to work on a worksheet or workbook?

8. How do you feel about going to school?

9. How do you feel about how well you read?

10. How do you think your friends feel about your reading?

Personal Report Card

Before formal reporting try inviting older students to write up their own report cards. Some teachers photocopy samples of actual report cards and have children fill them in. Or you can devise your own format (see Figure 7.6).

Figure 7.6 shows Jenni's personal report of how she felt she was progressing in sixth grade.

Name: Jennifer School: Grandview Grade Six Date May		
Principal ——————— Teacher ———————		
Rating : A outstanding ; B very good ; C average ; D little growth		
Subject	Grade	Comments
Listening	B	Jenni listens good in class, but is often caught talking to friends when she should be listening .
Speaking	B	Jenni speaks well by giving ideas and responding to ideas .
Reading	B +	Jenni reads a lot of good literature at her level . She does good literature responses and book talks
Writing Composing Process Spelling Mechanics	A + A B + A	Jenni composes excellent stories She is excellent in the process of writing and she revises most of her stories in her mind instead of revising on her paper and that's great! Jenni is a good speller and makes few mistakes. Jenni always (well almost) uses proper mechanics and is good at it.
		Report by Jenni

"Whole Language Behavior Inventory"

The "Whole Language Behavior Inventory" is in harmony with the developmental learning behaviors of students cited in research by Piaget, Tough, Holdaway, Beers, Gentry, and others. When we observe students in natural learning environments—listening to stories, playing with their friends in the sandbox or building area, reading literature, or developing a research chart—we notice that they develop proficiency in language at their own pace and level of development. The inventories in Tables 7.2, 7.3, and 7.4 show some of the common characteristics of language growth that you may observe your students experiencing as they progress from kindergarten to sixth grade.

Since students develop according to their own individual time clocks, which cannot be predetermined, the characteristics are not in any absolute order. Nor are the grade level indications absolute, since we know that students develop at different speeds. Past and present program strategies and language activities students have experienced also affect developmental growth. Students must have experienced dictation, for example, before they can dictate a composition of any length. Despite the uniqueness of each classroom and each child, the list of learning behaviors can guide teachers in observing the language development of their students.

REPORTING TO PARENTS AND
WHOLE LANGUAGE REPORT CARDS

All too often school districts implement whole language and continue to use traditional report cards. Since report cards appear to be a necessary evil in North America, we need at least to make them congruent with whole language philosophy. Principals can take a leadership role in bringing about necessary changes. First of all, the content designations usually need modification. Designations such as phonics, spelling, and handwriting should be removed since none are curriculum subject areas but rather subskills of reading and writing. Ideally, grades (both letter and numerical) ought also to be removed, since they compare child to child rather than indicate areas of strengths and weaknesses and strategies for continued growth. Report cards would be redundant if schools developed open-door policies where parents were invited to participate in the education of their children in a community school concept.

If we must use report cards, how should they look? These samples are alternatives you might consider. (*See* Tables 7.5–7.8.)

Table 7.2

Whole Language Behavior Inventory
Kindergarten–Grade One

Name: _____

Rating
N—no behavior
B—beginning
D—developing
S—secure

Date of Birth _____

Listening	Date/Rating	Speaking	Date/Rating
The student: distinguishes sounds in the environment listens to stories from books, records, films listens for new ideas listens to peers appreciates prose, poetry, rhyme listens for information comprehends facts, main ideas in discussion		The student: uses language to satisfy personal needs to give instructions, imagine, predict, project uses social language (greetings) describes objects and pictures narrates personal stories tells complete stories about one topic retells stories from literature sequences events in stories tells stories with expression uses sound effects in storytelling uses dialogue in storytelling dictates personal stories role-plays in variety of situations (alone or with others) uses telephone with familiar or imaginary person	

Reading	Date/Rating	Writing	Date/Rating
The student: enjoys listening to stories participates in shared reading activities looks at books as a self-initiated activity holds books right side up turns pages from front to back examines pictures in a book recalls the main idea of a familiar story recalls details from a familiar story can name events in a familiar story understands cause and effect in a familiar story predicts new ending to a familiar story uses pictures to gain meaning from text interprets stories through interpretive activities recognizes print in the environment (name, logos, signs) holds book and tells a story as though reading tells an appropriate story to match main idea of book		dictates information shares facts and information develops own grammar rules uses mature speech patterns COMPOSITION The student: communicates through talk communicates through drama and picture-making communicates through invented symbols (scribble, invented letters) dictates stories up to 5 sentences on one topic dictates stories up to 10 sentences on one topic composes narrative through scribble or invented letters composes narrative using conventional letters dictates poetry, letters, lists, pattern stories, reports writes from model sentence patterns labels with words labels with phrases over and under copies sentence strips writes series of pattern sentences (chaining)	

tells an appropriate story to match picture in a familiar book

holistically reconstructs a whole story to match a familiar story (story may not match exact text)

retells a refrain from a familiar story

retells with accuracy a repeated pattern in a book

attends to lines of print when attempting to reconstruct the story

retells a dictated story maintaining main idea

consistently turns pages left to right

attempts to match an oral story with each page of print as pages are turned

recognizes where print begins on a page

recognizes where print ends on a page

begins to move his or her eyes and finger left to right across the print while attempting to read (finger does not stop at individual words)

develops awareness of line directionality (child's finger moves left to right across line of print and then moves to the far left of the page and down to track the next line of print)

begins to point to clumps of letters and assigns an oral response (each oral

participates in group writing of poetry, letters, lists, pattern stories, and reports

writes according to model given by the teacher

dictates stories with series of events

composes fantasy stories recorded in print

SYMBOLIC REPRESENTATION

symbolizes stories through talk

symbolizes stories through drama

symbolizes stories through picture-making

symbolizes stories through dictation

symbolizes stories through random scribble

symbolizes stories with horizontal scribble

uses sentence scribble (one line of scribble represents a sentence)

uses word scribble (scribble is broken into segments to represent words)

uses invented letters (N for H)

uses upper-case letters

integrates scribble symbols with conventional letters

uses predominance of conventional letters (upper and lower case) response may not accurately match the text)

reads own page of big book

begins to track (point to individual words) in a familiar story

tracks accurately first and last word of a sentence strip

tracks accurately all words in a single sentence strip or sentence pattern

tracks to find a specific word

uses pictures, pattern, semantics, and syntax to gain meaning

recognizes common words in stories

can recognize up to 5 words in a sentence strip

can recognize up to 5 words in a familiar pattern literature selection

can recognize up to 5 words from a dictated story immediately after dictation

tracks accurately several sentences in a familiar story

tracks accurately two or more sentences in a dictated story immediately after dictation

reads any page in familiar big book

uses memory, pictures to gain meaning from a familiar text

uses memory, pictures, syntax pattern to

---

may use typewriter or computer print

SPELLING

uses scribble to represent spelling

uses random letters to represent words

uses conventional letters but no sound-symbol relationships

uses letter-name spelling (*m* for *am*, *n* for *and*)

uses initial consonant spelling (I w s l n; I went skating last night)

uses initial and final consonant spelling (I wt s lt nt)

uses temporary spellings (I wnt sktg lst nit)

spells high-frequency words conventionally (name, to, a, and, the)

begins to make the transition from temporary to conventional spelling (oo, w, wt, wnt, went)

one quarter of story has conventional spelling

CONVENTIONS

prints scribble or letters horizontally left to right across the page

leaves spaces between words

uses "and" as placeholder for punctuation

begins to use punctuation at the end of lines

gain meaning from a familiar text
uses memory, pictures, pattern, and tracking to gain meaning from a familiar text
accurately reads a sentence strip recently dictated
accurately reads up to 5 familiar sentence strips
accurately reads 2 or 3 familiar pattern books
accurately reads 5 familiar pattern books
reads up to 10 familiar pattern books
tracks current dictated story with some accurate word matching
tracks current dictated story with much accurate word matching
tracks current dictated story with almost accurate word matching
reads familiar charts
tracks old dictated stories with some accuracy
tracks old dictated stories with much accuracy
becomes aware of letter and sound-symbol relationships
uses phonetic cues with familiar material
reads numerous familiar pattern texts with accuracy

overgeneralizes punctuation
uses upper-and-lower case letters indiscriminately
uses capital letter for beginning of name
uses capital letters for beginning of names of friends

REVISING
rarely revises
will consider minor additions to dictated stories providing you scribe the changes
may allow cosmetic changes to written stories
may suggest minor additions to stories before publication
may add information at the end of first draft
resists deleting information from a story
resists re-organizing a story

EDITING
prefers written stories to be published as is and not to be edited into standard print
may allow some minor editing of the story providing the teacher does it

PUBLISHING
prefers an adult to print or type the final copy

begins to read new predictable pattern books with some accuracy uses picture clues, syntax, tracking, memory, and semantics to gain meaning uses picture clues, syntax tracking, memory, semantics, and phonics to gain meaning from new predictable pattern books begins to self-correct reading reads new pattern literature with ease reads current dictated stories (5 to 10 sentences) reads own published dictated stories appreciates favorite authors reads grade level text (grade one)	prefers to publish dictation rather than personal writing

Table 7.3

Whole Language Behavior Inventory
Grades Two and Three

Name: _____

Rating
N—no behavior
B—beginning
D—developing
S—secure

Date of Birth _____

Listening	Date/Rating	Speaking	Date/Rating
The student: sustains listening in two-way conversations is sensitive to detail of sounds in environment and sounds in language hears main idea and story sequence appreciates prose, poetry, song compares relationships in prose and poetry comprehends facts, details, main idea in print makes predictions through discussions listens for oral directions		The student: uses language to satisfy personal needs to give instructions, imagine, reason, predict, project, hypothesize uses social language (greetings, introductions) uses more complex language (sentence variety, descriptive vocabulary) argues, discusses different points of view dramatizes characters using movement and language retells folk tales uses sound effects in retelling reports news, observations, and information dictates personal stories of more than 10 sentences dictates information	

dictates fantasy
dictates in groups
is aware of speaking behavior (being polite, listening to others, taking turns)
uses telephone with friends and family

Writing

COMPOSITION
The student:
dictates up to 10 sentences about one topic
dictates up to 20 sentences about one topic
writes 5–10 sentence stories
writes 10–20 sentence stories
dictates narrative, fantasy, poetry, letters, lists, pattern stories
models reports, riddles, poetry, folk tales
dictates stories with characters, setting, action, conclusions, and logical sequence
uses dialogue in dictated stories
uses dialogue in written stories
writes narrative
writes fantasy stories
writes bed-to-bed stories (I got up, had breakfast . . . went out for recess . . .

Reading

The student:
participates in shared reading activities
enjoys listening to stories
enjoys interpreting picture books
reads familiar pattern literature
can read much of personal dictated stories and charts
reads personal dictated stories and charts with understanding
reads own published books
reads new pattern literature and dictation through discussion
comprehends main idea, details, inferences in discussions
interprets pattern stories through interpretive activities (art, drama)
reads material at grade level
reads narrative, fantasy, and factual material at grade level

had supper and went to bed)

writes stories consisting of a list of
events

writes poetry, letters, lists, pattern
stories, riddles, folk tales

SYMBOLIC REPRESENTATION

The student:

symbolizes stories through talk, drama,
and dictation

symbolizes stories through scribble,
invented letters

symbolizes stories with conventional
letters (upper and lower case)

uses cursive writing

uses typewriter

uses word processor

SPELLING

begins to recognize unconventional
spellings

begins to self-correct spelling

CONVENTIONS

PUNCTUATION

is inconsistent in use of punctuation

overgeneralizes rules of punctuation

uses "and" as place holder for
punctuation

uses periods consistently at end of
thoughts

uses presodics to indicate expression
begins to use quotation marks

CAPITALIZATION

overgeneralizes capitals
puts capitals at beginning of sentences
uses capitals for names of people
begins to put capitals for names of places
begins to put capitals on initials and titles
usually uses capitals appropriately

GRAMMAR

understands contractions
understands possessives

REVISING

will make changes in composition of dictation
will make changes in composition of written stories
will add information to end of story
will add descriptive language
will add information to body of story
will revise content in stories once or twice
may reorganize story with adult assistance
begins to use conference techniques with self and peers
will occasionally delete information from stories

EDITING

will edit conventions for self
  (punctuation, capitalization, spelling)
will circle items he or she is unsure of
will edit for peers at peer editing center

PUBLISHING

enjoys publishing dictated stories
enjoys publishing written stories
prefers an adult to retype final copy
will publish in different formats
  (booklets, charts, banners, posters,
  etc.)

Table 7.4

Whole Language Behavior Inventory
Grades Four to Six

Name: _____

Rating
N—no behavior
B—beginning
D—developing
S—secure

Date of Birth _____

Listening	Date/Rating	Speaking	Date/Rating
The student: listens critically in conversations (extends or sees flaws in discussion) listens for story development (setting, theme, characters, problems, and conclusions) listens for specific purposes (appreciation, critical, information) listens for oral directions comprehends facts, details, ideas, and predicts, compares, and analyzes through discussions listens in group activities		The student: uses language to satisfy personal needs to give instructions, imagine, reason, predict, project, hypothesize, analyze uses social language confidently (introductions, greetings, thank you's) uses more complex language (sentences, description, dialogue) debates, discusses, convinces, interviews dramatizes whole stories using movement, language, art, music retells folk tales using props reports news, information, observations with organization dictates personal stories, narratives, fantasy, fairy tales, and information edits dictations orally	

Reading	Date/Rating	Writing	Date/Rating
		uses telephone with friends, family uses telephone to seek information	

Reading	Date/Rating	Writing	Date/Rating
The student: enjoys being involved in readers' theater (dramatized readings) enjoys listening to literature reads own dictated stories reads dictated stories of others reads variety of factual material (newspapers, maps, brochures) reads charts reads published books of classmates reads literature at grade level comprehends main idea, details critically analyzes selections reads factual material at grade level self selects literature appropriately chooses to read as an activity reads a variety of genre (realistic, fantasy, fairy tales, poetry, fables, myths, mystery novels)		COMPOSITION The student: dictates 10–20 sentences about one topic dictates more than 30 sentences about one topic writes 10 sentence stories writes 10–20 sentence stories writes 20–30 sentence stories dictates narrative, fantasy, poetry, letters, reports, riddles writes narratives, fantasy, poetry, letters, reports models legends, myths, fables, folk tales in group writing writes bed-to-bed stories (I got up, I had breakfast, I went to school, came home, had supper, and went to bed) writes stories consisting of listing of events writes legends, myths, fables, folk tales writes stories with setting, characters, action, plot, logical conclusions is able to focus story on one episode uses dialogue and descriptive language	

SYMBOLIC REPRESENTATION

symbolizes through drama
symbolizes through pictures and print
symbolizes through dictation
uses varieties of manuscript print
uses cursive writing
uses diagrams
uses charts
uses typewriters
uses word processor
uses calligraphy

SPELLING

no longer uses letter name spellings
no longer uses consonant spellings
sometimes uses temporary spellings for
   difficult words (becuze for because)
uses a predominance of conventional
   spelling
uses dictionaries to edit spelling

CONVENTIONS

PUNCTUATION

uses periods appropriately
uses question marks appropriately
uses exclamation marks appropriately
uses quotation marks accurately
is aware of commas, dashes

CAPITALIZATION
uses capitals appropriately for:
  the beginning of sentences
  names of people
  names of places
  initials
  titles

GRAMMAR
understands possessives
understands contractions

REVISION
will make changes in the composition of
  dictated stories
will make changes in the composition of
  written stories
will add information to the end of
  stories
will add information to body of stories
will add descriptive detail
will reorganize events in story
will delete redundant material from
  story
will redraft once
will redraft twice or three times
will redraft more than three times
participates in conferences
uses conference techniques for self and
  peers

EDITING

will edit conventions for self (spelling, punctuation)

will circle aspects he or she is unsure of

will edit conventions for peers in an editing team

uses dictionary, thesaurus in editing

PUBLISHING

prefers to have published stories typed by parent, teacher, or volunteer

will publish in a variety of ways (booklet, tape or slide, wall hangings)

Table 7.5
Anecdotal Report

Term _____	School _____
Name _____	Grade _____
Date _____	Teacher _____

Comments

Social/Emotional Development

Language Arts
  Listening

  Speaking

  Reading

  Writing

Environmental Studies

Mathematics

The Arts (Physical Education, Music, Art)

_____   _____

Principal's Signature   Teacher's Signature

Table 7.6
Anecdotal Checklist Report

Name _____	Date _____
School _____	Teacher _____
Grade _____	Principal _____

Comments

Listening/Speaking
  listens to stories
  discusses meaning of stories
  tells and dictates stories
Reading Development
  recognizes print symbols
  demonstrates directionality
  chooses books for self
  emergent stage
  beginning stage
  independent stage
  reads at grade level
  uses variety of cueing strategies (pictures,
      syntax, context, phonetic)
  comprehends by retelling
  comprehends in writing
Writing
  dictates stories
  writes first drafts
  symbols used (picture, scribble, letters)
  spelling (consonants, invented, conventional)
  conventions (punctuation, grammar)
  revises
  edits
  publishes
The Arts
  responds in visual arts
  enjoys music activities
  participates in physical education
Environmental Studies
  shares knowledge of the environment
  uses problem-solving skills
Mathematics
  demonstrates arithmetic skills
  demonstrates measurement skills
  demonstrates geometry skills

Table 7.7
Checklist—Comment Report

Name _____	Date _____
School _____	Principal _____
Grade _____	Teacher _____

Characteristics of student behavior

1. Demonstrates unusual strength	3. Receives additional support
2. Developmentally appropriate	4. Requires special assistance

	Comments	*Rating*
Listening		
(recreational and informational)		
Speaking		
(storytelling, discussions, dictation, reporting)		
Reading		
developmental stage		
fiction/nonfiction		
comprehension (retelling)		
cueing strategies		
reads dictated stories		
reads at grade level		
Writing		
dictates personal stories		
writes first drafts		
writes for variety of genre		
revises content		
spelling development		
conventions (punctuation, grammar)		
edits/publishes		
The Arts		
visual art		
music		
physical education		
Environmental Studies		
(social studies, science, geography, history)		
Mathematics		
Arithmetic/Geometry		
Measurement		
Fine Motor		
(construction, drawing, handwriting)		

Table 7.8
Checklist Report

Name _____	Date _____
School _____	Teacher _____
Grade _____	Principal _____

Characteristics of student behavior

1. Demonstrates unusual strength   3. Receives additional support
2. Developmentally appropriate   4. Requires special assistance

	Rating		Rating

Social-Emotional
   Self-confident; tries new
     activities; co-operates;
     works independently
 Fine Motor Skills
   Shows fine muscle co-
     ordination in art and in
     handwriting
 The Arts
   Responds in visual arts;
     enjoys music activities;
     participates in physical
     education
 Environmental Studies
   Shares knowledge of
     environment and uses
     problem-solving skills
 _____
 	
 Comments
		Language Arts
		 Listening
		   Listens to stories
		   Listens to instruction
		 Speaking
		   communicates ideas
		 Reading
		   shows interest in literature
		   reads appropriate to stage
		     of development
		   reads dictated stories
		   reads variety of fact and
		     fiction
		   comprehends in retelling
		   comprehends in writing
		   uses variety of cueing
		     strategies
		   reads at grade level
		 Writing
		   dictates stories
		   writes first drafts
		   revises
		   develops conventions
		     (spelling, phonics,
		     grammar)
		   edits
		   publishes
		 Mathematics
		   demonstrates arithmetic
		     skills
		   demonstrates measurement
		     skills
		   demonstrates geometry
		     skills	

Teacher's Signature	Principal's Signature		

8. Whole Language Research: Key Studies and Reference Literature

Principals interested in implementing whole language want to know the various studies that support whole language philosophy. Only a few of the pertinent studies are listed here, along with references that can be obtained for in-depth reading. The studies are organized according to general headings:

Developmental Interactive Learning
Oral Language
Reading
Writing

Within each section key research is cited by author and is followed by referenced bibliography indicating where the research reports can be located. This outline can be used by your teachers to gain background about research in language learning; as a reference for you to gain whole language support from your superintendent; or as a list to refer to when responding to parental questions.

RESOURCE MATERIALS FOR WHOLE LANGUAGE

Implementing whole language requires obtaining resources for your teachers that will be both theoretical and practical in nature. Try to provide both types of information for your staff so as to accommodate the various ways in which teachers learn. Some teachers, for example, prefer to read all about the theory first before they attempt the practice, while others will want to try out various strategies before reading about theoretical implications. The following resources are listed with these learning styles in mind:

Whole language theory and research books
Whole language teacher resource books
Classroom materials.

Remember to take an inventory of the resources you already own or can borrow before you purchase new items.

Table 8.1
Developmental Interactive Learning Research

Research Focus	Researchers	Synopsis of Research	References
Emergent literacy	M.J.M. Baghban (1984)	Baghban conducted a detailed longitudinal case study of his daughter from age one to three that indicated her knowledge of a multitude of reading and writing behaviors.	Baghban, M.J.M. *Our Daughter Learns to Read and Write: A Case Study from Birth to Three,* Newark, DE: International Reading Association, 1984.
Preschool literacy	Marie Clay (1975); Holdaway (1979); Ferreiro & Teberosky (1982); Harste, Woodward and Burke (1984)	All of these researchers have documented evidence that pre-school children have a wealth of literate knowledge in oral language, reading and writing before they come to school.	Clay, Marie. *What Did I Write?* London: Heinemann Educational Books, 1975. Holdaway, Don. *Foundations of Literacy.* Toronto: Ashton Scholastic, 1979. Ferreiro, Emelia, and Anna Teberosky. *Literacy before Schooling.* Portsmouth, N.H.: Heinemann Educational Books, 1982. Harste, Jerome C., Virginia A. Woodward, and Carolyn Burke. *Language Stories and Literacy Lessons.* Portsmouth, N.H.: Heinemann Educational Books, 1984.

Criticism of skills-based basals	Kenneth Goodman (1964)	Goodman's research (1964) is critical of language instruction based on hierarchies of skills, and argues that children learn language in a complex integrative, interactive way by using contextual, syntactical, and phonetic cues.	Goodman, Kenneth. "Effective Teachers of Reading Know Language and Children." *Elementary English*, vol. 51, no. 6 (Sept. 1974).
Criticism of skills-based basals	Kenneth Goodman, Patrick Shannon, Yvonne Freeman, and Sharon Murphy (1988)	NCTE Commission on Reading Study of Basals. It examines the history, philosophy, and economics of basals, teaching strategies, testing methods, and more.	Goodman, Kenneth, Patrick Shannon, Yvonne Freeman, and Sharon Murphy, *Report Card on Basal Readers*. Katonah, N.Y.: Richard C. Owen Publishers, 1988.
Complexity of language learning	Frank Smith (1969)	Smith's research on young fluent readers indicates that language learning (listening, speaking, reading, and writing) is a complex process that youngsters learn as they are engaged in actual acts of speaking, reading, and writing.	Smith, Frank. *Understanding Reading*. Toronto: Holt, Rinehart and Winston, 1971.
Emergent literacy	Elizabeth Sulzby and William Teale (1987)	Sulzby and Teele's investigations of the emergent reader and writer offer in-depth data on developmental language behavior.	Sulzby, Elizabeth, and William Teale. *Emergent Literacy: Writing and Reading*. Norwood, N.J.: Ablex, 1987.
Integration of listening, speaking, reading, and writing	Elizabeth Thorn (1974)	Thorn's research in Canada demonstrates that listening, speaking, reading, and writing are mutually supportive in language learning.	Thorn, Elizabeth. *Teaching the Language Arts*. Toronto: Gage Educational Publishing, 1974.

Table 8.2
Oral Language Research

Research Focus	Researchers	Synopsis of Research	References
Oral language acquisition	J. Aitchison (1973)	Aitchison's research in Britain demonstrated that children's oral language grows developmentally rather than from formal instruction.	Aitchison, J. *Articulate Mammal.* London: Hutchinson, 1973.
	Carol Chomsky (1969)	Chomsky's research with oral language development of pre-schoolers showed that children learn to speak as they actively engage in communication, rather than through formal instruction, and that rules of oral grammar are also acquired developmentally and not taught.	Chomsky, Carol. *The Acquisition of Syntax from 5 to 10.* Cambridge, MA: MIT Press, 1969. Chomsky, Carol. "Stages in Language Development and Reading Exposure," *Harvard Educational Review,* vol. 41, no. 1 (Feb. 1972).
Functions of language	Michael Halliday (1970–1975)	Halliday, in the study of his son's oral language development in England, observed the key functions of speech a child uses.	Halliday, Michael. *Learning How to Mean.* London: Arnold, 1975.
Oral language acquisition across cultures	Dan Slobin (1985)	Slobin, in Berkeley, California, is involved with researchers from many parts of the world studying similarities in language acquisition across cultures.	Slobin, Dan. *The Cross-linguistic Study of Language Acquisition,* D. Sloban, ed. Hillsdale, N.J.: Erlbaum, 1985.
Oral interactions between pupils and teachers	Vera Southgate, Helen Arnold, and Sandra Johnson (1979)	In research in England of seven- to nine-year-olds, Southgate *et al.* discovered that the length of most oral interactions with an individual pupil was 30 seconds or less.	Southgate, Vera, Helen Arnold, and Sandra Johnson. *Extending Beginning Reading.* London: Heinemann Educational Books, 1981.

Comparative study of oral language at home *vs.* oral language at school	Gordon Wells (1973–1979)	Wells' longitudinal study from pre-school to third grade of oral language development of 32 children in Bristol, England, demonstrated that oral language of the child was superior in the home compared to the school context with regard to the amount of utterances a child makes, turns in conversation a child has, types of meaning expressed by the child, numbers of interactions of conversation, and proportion of questions asked.	Wells, Gordon. *Language Development in the Pre-school Years.* Cambridge: Cambridge University Press, 1985.
Developmental sequence of oral language behavior	Gordon Wells (1973–1979)	Wells' research in oral language development of pre-schoolers in England provides a full account of the sequence of development in oral language. ("Language Development in Pre-School Years," 1985).	Wells, Gordon. *The Meaning Makers.* N.H.: Heinemann Educational Books, 1986.
Teacher talk	David Wood, L. McMahon, and Y. Cranstoun (1980)	Wood *et al.'s* research in England found that 44 percent of teacher talk was concerned with management.	Wood, David, L. McMahon, and Y. Cranstoun. *Working with Under Fives.* London: Grant McIntyre, 1980.

Table 8.3
Reading Research

Research Focus	Researchers	Synopsis of Research	References
Word learning	Richard Allington and Anne McGill-Frazen	Richard Allington and Anne McGill-Frazen in their research on word identification errors found that both good and poor readers were helped most by context rather than in isolation, and concluded that a child's performance on word lists is not a good predictor of which words might be missed in context.	Allington, Richard L., and Anne McGill-Frazen. "Word Identification, Errors in Isolation and in Context: Apples vs. Oranges." *The Reading Teacher*, 33, 795–800 (April 1980).
Basal text deficiencies	Bruno Bettelheim and K. Zelan (1979–1980)	Bettelheim and Zelan's study of reading materials in the U.S. (1982) showed that these lacked real literature, were contrived, and were often uninteresting.	Bettelheim, B., and K. Zelan. *On Listening to Read*. N.Y.: Knopf, 1981.
Reading sight vocabulary	Connie Bridge *et al.* (1983)	Connie Bridge and associates showed that kindergarten children and low-achieving first-graders learned more sight words using predictable storybooks than using skill-based reading readiness basals.	Bridge, C.A., P.N. Winogra, and D. Haley. "Using Predictable Materials to Teach Beginning Reading." *The Reading Teacher*, 36, 884–891, 1983.
Reading phonics instruction	Marie Carbo (1987)	Marie Carbo's reading styles research concluded that only a small percentage of children really need phonics instruction to become good readers.	Carbo, Marie. "Reading Styles Research: What Works Isn't Always Phonics." *Phi Delta Kappan*, 68, 431–435, 1987.
Phonetics retards reading growth	Marie Clay (1967)	Clay's research in New Zealand showed that mature readers don't use phonetic cueing systems, and that over-reliance on the phonetic strategy retards reading progress.	Clay, Marie M. *Reading: The Patterning of Complex Behaviour*. London: Heinemann, 1977.

Natural language texts	Marie Clay (1967)	Clay's research indicated that children read more easily when the texts retained the qualities of the child's natural oral language, was predictable, and had literary quality.	
Emergent reading behavior	Marie Clay (1967–1970)	Clay's three-year longitudinal study of emergent readers in New Zealand resulted in descriptions of emergent reading behaviors.	
Comparative study—basals *vs.* shared reading	David Doake (1977–1980)	Doake's research comparing basal reading approaches to shared reading approaches showed that children in shared reading had more advanced growth in comprehension and vocabulary than children taught with basals.	Doake, David. "Book Experience and Emergent Reading Behavior." Paper presented at the Preconvention Institute, International Reading Association Annual Convention, Atlanta, GA (April 1979). Doake, David. *Report on the Shared Book Experience Approach to Learning to Read.* Wolfville, Nova Scotia: Arcadia University School of Education (April 1980).
Preschool readers read naturally	Dolores Durkin (1965)	Durkin's study of pre-school readers indicated that children could learn to read naturally, providing the environment was stimulating, literate, and secure.	Durkin, Dolores. *Children Who Read Early.* N.Y.: Teachers College Press, 1966.
Reading story books for reading in ESL	Warwick, Elley, and Francis Mangubhai (1983)	Elley and Mangubhai studied 380 nine- to eleven-year-olds learning to read English as a second language using storybooks rather than skills-oriented basals. Standardized test results in reading and listening comprehension progressed at twice the normal rate.	Elley, Warwick B., and Francis Mangubhai. "The Impact of Reading on Second Language Learning." *Reading Research Quarterly,* 19, 53–67 (Fall 1983).

Environmental print awareness in South American children	Emilia Ferreiro and Anna Teberosky (1976–1981)	Ferreiro and Teberosky's research in South America (1982) shows that in a literate society children become aware of environmental print developmentally, not through direct instruction.	Ferreiro, Emilia, and Anna Teberosky. *Literacy before Schooling.* Portsmouth, N.H.: Heinemann Educational Books, 1982.
Pre-school print awareness	Yetta Goodman (1976–1980)	Goodman's research on pre-schoolers indicated that children are aware of print before they come to school.	Goodman, K.S. "Effective Teachers of Reading Know Language and Children." *Elementary English,* vol. 51, no. 6 (Sept. 1974). Goodman, Yetta. *A Model of Beginning Reading: The Roots of Literacy.* Arizona Center for Research and Development, University of Arizona, 1980.
Reading print knowledge	Elfrieda Hiebert (1981)	Hiebert assessed three-, four- and five-year-olds' knowledge of purposes and processes in reading and discovered that they were aware of print.	Hiebert, E.H. "Developmental Patterns and Interrelationships of Preschool Children's Print Awareness." *Reading Research Quarterly,* 16, 236–260, 1981.
Reading without formal instruction	Don Holdaway (1976–1979); David Doake (1975–1980)	Don Holdaway's studies in New Zealand and David Doake's investigations in Canada of pre-school children learning to read showed that young children can learn to read without formal instruction when they are exposed regularly to quality literature and invited to read along.	Don Holdaway. *Foundations of Literacy.* Toronto: Ashton Scholastic, 1979. Don Holdaway. *Independence in Reading.* Toronto: Ashton Scholastic, 1980. David Doake. *Report on the Shared Book Experience Approach to Learning to Read.* Wolfville, Nova Scotia: Acadia University School of Education (April 1980).
Basal text deficiencies	J. Lutz (1974)	Lutz's study in the U.S. of twenty-five basal texts in primary grades indicated that sentences were simple, monotonous, short, and sterile.	Lutz, J. "Some Comments on Psycholinguistic Research and Education." *The Reading Teacher* (Oct. 1974).

Reading comprehension	Michael Sampson *et al.* (1982)	Sampson and his colleagues compared basal stories to dictated stories of first grade students and found that the mean language level of the dictation was higher than the basal stories, and that students were able to process and comprehend the student-authored stories better than the basals.	Sampson, M.R., and J. White. "The Effect of Student-authored Materials on the Performance of Beginning Readers." Paper presented at the thirty-second annual meeting of the National Reading Conference, Clearwater, FL, 1982.
Interference of word study in reading	Frank Smith (1965–1969)	Smith's Canadian research with fluent readers in 1969 demonstrated that isolated vocabulary study interfered with meaning because many words have different meanings.	Frank Smith. *Psycholinguistics and Reading.* N.Y.: Holt, Rinehart and Winston, 1973.
Comparative study: basal *vs.* language experience	Russell G. Stauffer (1960–1965)	Stauffer's research in language experience, comparing the language experience approach to the basal approach (1965), showed that children from the language experience approach earned higher scores in paragraph meaning, spelling, reading, and writing than children taught with the basal.	Stauffer, Russell G. *The Language Experience Approach to the Teaching of Reading.* N.Y.: Harper & Row, 1970.
Storybooks for reading	Elizabeth Sulzby (1985)	Sulzby's research on kindergarten children using storybooks as reading material showed improved reading ability, and indicated several stages of reading behaviors.	Sulzby, Elizabeth. "Children's Emergent Reading of Favourite Story Books: A Development Study." *Reading Research Quarterly,* 20, 458–481 (Summer 1985).

Table 8.4
Writing Research

Research Focus	Researchers	Synopsis of Research	References
Concept of story	Arthur Applebee (1975–1977)	Applebee's writing research gives us insights into the child's concept of composing a story.	Applebee, Arthur. *The Child's Concept of Story Ages Two to Seventeen.* Chicago: University of Chicago Press, 1978.
Case study of a child's writing over 5 years	Glenda Bissex (1972–1979)	Bissex studied her son Paul's writing progress over five years and gathered in-depth data about the writing process.	Bissex, Glenda. *GNYS AT WRK: A Child Learns to Write and Read.* Cambridge, MA: Harvard University Press, 1980.
Writing mechanics development	Lucy Calkins (1980)	Calkins compared the learning of mechanics by third-grade children in a process-writing classroom, and discovered that skills of mechanics were more effectively learned in context than in isolation.	Calkins, Lucy McCormick. "When Children Want to Punctuate: Basic Skills Belong in Context." *Language Arts,* 57, 567–573 (May 1980).
Developmental growth of two students	Brian Cambourne and Jan Turbill (1985–1987)	Cambourne and Turbill's study in the Warrawong schools, Queensland, Australia, reports developmental growth in writing of ESL and English-speaking first-graders.	Cambourne, B., and J. Turbill. *Coping with Chaos.* Australia: Primary English Teaching Association, 1987.
Invented spelling	Carol Chomsky (1968–1969)	Chomsky's studies (1971) of children's writing indicated that spelling development begins with spelling approximations, but that these approximations gradually become accurate when students have ample opportunities to write.	Chomsky, Carol. "Write First, Read Later." *Childhood Education,* vol. 47, no. 6 (1971).
Scribble in the writing process	Marie Clay (1972–1974)	Clay's investigation of pre-school writers showed that children demonstrate story through drawings, scribble, and invented letters.	Clay, Marie. *What Did I Write?* London: Heinemann Educational Books, 1975.

Implications of drawing and scribble on writing process	Diane De Ford (1977–1978)	De Ford's research of 50 two- to seven-year-olds' writings indicate that children communicate messages from drawings and scribble before they are concerned with conventional letters.	De Ford, Diane E. "Young Children and Their Writing." *Theory into Practice,* vol. 19, no. 3 (Summer 1980).
Writing in skills-based programs *vs.* whole language program	Diane De Ford (1981)	Diane De Ford compared reading and writing in a phonics classroom, a skills classroom and a whole language classroom, and discovered that in the phonics and skills classrooms, where the environment was print-restricted, children's writing growth was inhibited; in the whole language classroom with a print-rich environment, writing was facilitated.	De Ford, Diane E. "Literacy: Reading, Writing and Other Essentials." *Language Arts,* 58, 652–658 (Sept. 1981).
Scribble in first-grade writing	B. Gail Heald-Taylor (1981–1983)	Heald-Taylor's research of first-grade writers revealed children use scribble in a variety of ways to intend meaning of story, sentence, and word.	Heald-Taylor, B. Gail. "Reading and Writing: The Natural Language Approach from Theory to Practice." Unpublished Master's Project, College of Education, Brock University, St. Catharines, Ontario, Canada, 1983. Heald-Taylor, B. Gail. "Scribble in First Grade Writing." *The Reading Teacher,* vol. 38, no. 1 (Oct. 1984).
Writing process of twelfth-grade students	Janet Emig (1960–1969)	Emig's U.S. study of the composing processes of twelfth-grade students pioneered work in the case-study research approach to writing, and described components of the writing process of twelfth-grade students.	Emig, Janet. "Components of the Composing Process among Twelfth Grade Writers." Doctoral Dissertation, Harvard University, 1969. Emig, Janet. "Non-magical Thinking: Presenting Writing Developmentally in Schools." In *Writing:*

			Process Development and Communication. vol. 11, C. Frederickson and J. Dominic, eds. Hillsdale, N.J.: Erlbaum, 1981.
Dearth of research writing	Donald Graves (1976–1979)	Graves studied the relationship between reading and writing, and gave insights into: how impoverished American basal textbooks are in the area of writing; how writing time in American curricula is shortchanged compared to time provided for reading.	Graves, Donald. *Balance the Basics: Let Them Write*. N.Y.: Ford Foundation, 1978.
Sex differences in writing; writing process of seven-year-olds; teacher dependency in writing; relationships between reading and writing; writing impoverished textbooks; writing time in American schools	Donald Graves (1972–1985)	Graves' various research projects have provided a wealth of data resulting in profound implications for writing practices in American classrooms. Graves' doctoral study (1972–1976) of seven-year-olds' writing provides information about: sex differences in children's writing; the role of the professional in the writing process; an examination of the writing processes of seven-year-old children; how teachers make children dependent upon them in the writing process.	Graves, Donald. "The Growth and Development of First Grade Writers." Paper presented at the Canadian Council of Teachers of English Annual Meeting. Ottawa, May 1979. Graves, Donald. *A Researcher Learns to Write*. Exeter, N.H.: Heinemann Educational Books, 1984.
Writing process	Donald Graves, Lucy McCormick Calkins, and Susan Sowers (1978–1982)	Atkinson, New Hampshire Study by Graves, Calkins, and Sowers conducted over three years of writing processes of first- to third-grade writers. Their work provided research on: the importance of observing children in the process of writing to learn how the writing process works;	Lucy McCormick Calkins. "Children's Rewriting Strategies." *Research in the Teaching of English*, vol. 14 (Dec. 1980).

how teachers support children in the revising process through conferences.

Correlation between grammar instruction and writing	R. Koch (1978–1980)	Koch's research demonstrated that there is no correlation between the teaching of grammar and improvement in writing.	Koch, R. "Syllogisms and Superstitions: The Current State of Responding to Writing." *Language Arts,* vol. 59, no. 5 (May 1982).
Lack of writing across the curriculum	N. Martin, P. D'Arcy, B. Newton, and R. Parker (1974–1975)	Martin *et al.*'s British study of writing across the high-school curriculum indicated that in subjects other than English there is little opportunity for storytelling or story writing.	Martin, N., P. D'Arcy, B. Newton, and R. Parker. *Writing and Learning across the Curriculum.* London: Ward Lock Educational, 1976.
Learning to write by experimentation	Charles Temple, Ruth G. Nathan, and Nancy Burris (1975–1978)	Temple *et al.*'s studies show that children learn to write by experimenting and discovery, rather than by being formally taught.	Temple, Charles, Ruth G. Nathan, and Nancy Burris. *The Beginnings of Writing.* Toronto: Allyn & Bacon, 1982.

Table 8.5
Comparative Research

Research Focus	Researchers	Synopsis of Research	References
Whole language and test scores	Lucy Calkins (1982)	In research at Atkinson Academy, where teachers predominantly used whole language strategies, achievement on the Iowa Test of Basic Skills rose twenty-seven points during the past seven years.	Calkins, Lucy McCormick. "Writing Taps a New Energy." *The Child. Donald Graves in Australia.* R.D. Walsh, ed. Portsmouth, N.H.: Heinemann, 45–54 (1982).
Whole language and test scores	Margaret Phinney (1986)	In Phinney's informal research one class of children was tracked for three years in whole language classroom environments. Significant gains were made on the Canadian Test of Basic Skills.	Phinney, Margaret. Unpublished report (1986).

Table 8.6

Whole Language Theory and Research Books

Developmental Interactive Learning	
Clay, Marie	*What Did I Write?* London: Heinemann Educational Books, 1975.
Ferreiro, Emelia, and Anna Teberosky	*Literacy before Schooling.* Portsmouth, N.H.: Heinemann Educational Books, 1982.
Goodman, Kenneth	"Effective Teachers of Reading Know Language and Children." *Elementary English*, vol. 51, no. 6 (Sept. 1974).
Harste, Jerome C., Virginia A. Woodward, and Carolyn Burke	*Language Stories and Literacy Lessons.* Portsmouth, N.H.: Heinemann Educational Books, 1984.
Holdaway, Don	*Foundations of Literacy.* Sydney N.S.W.: Ashton Scholastic, 1979.
Smith, Frank	*Understanding Reading.* Toronto: Holt, Rinehart and Winston, 1971.
Sulzby, Elizabeth, and William Teale	*Emergent Literacy: Writing and Reading.* Norwood, N.J.: Ablex, 1987.
Thorn, Elizabeth	*Teaching the Language Arts.* Toronto: Gage Educational Publishing, 1974.

Oral Language Research	
Aitchison, J.	*Articulate Mammal.* London: Hutchinson, 1973.
Chomsky, Carol	*The Acquisition of Syntax from 5 to 10.* Cambridge, MA: MIT Press, 1969.
Chomsky, Carol	"Stages in Language Development and Reading Exposure," *Harvard Educational Review*, vol. 41, no. 1 (Feb. 1972).
Halliday, Michael	*Learning How to Mean.* London: Arnold, 1975.
Slobin, Dan	*The Cross-Linguistic Study of Language Acquisition*, D. Slobin, ed. Hillsdale, N.J.: Erlbaum, 1985.
Southgate, Vera, Helen Arnold, and Sandra Johnson	*Extending Beginning Reading.* London: Heinemann Educational Books, 1981.
Wells, Gordon	*Language Development in the Pre-school Years.* Cambridge: Cambridge University Press, 1985.
Wells, Gordon	*The Meaning Makers.* N.H.: Heinemann Educational Books, 1986.

Wood, David, L. McMahon, and Y. Cranstoun	*Working with Under Fives*. London: Grant McIntyre, 1980.

Reading Research

Bettelheim, B., and K. Zelan	*On Learning to Read*. N.Y.: Knopf, 1981.
Clay, Marie	*Reading: The Patterning of Complex Behaviour*. London: Heinemann Ltd., 1977.
Doake, David	"Book Experience and Emergent Reading Behaviour." Paper presented at the Preconvention Institute, International Reading Association Annual Convention. Atlanta, GA (April 1979).
Doake, David	*Report on the Shared Book Experience Approach to Learning to Read*. Wolfville, Nova Scotia: Acadia University School of Education (April 1980).
Durkin, Dolores	*Children Who Read Early*. N.Y.: Teachers College Press, 1966.
Ferreiro, Emilia, and Anna Teberosky	*Literacy before Schooling*. Portsmouth, N.H.: Heinemann Educational Books, 1982.
Goodman, K.S.	"Effective Teachers of Reading Know Language and Children." *Elementary English*, vol. 51, no. 6 (Sept. 1974).
Goodman, Yetta	*A Model of Beginning Reading: The Roots of Literacy*. Arizona Center for Research and Development, University of Arizona, 1980.
Holdaway, Don	*Foundations of Literacy*. Sydney N.S.W.: Ashton Scholastic, 1979.
Holdaway, Don	*Independence in Reading*. Ashton Scholastic, 1980.
Lutz, J.	"Some Comments on Psycholinguistic Research and Education." *The Reading Teacher* (Oct. 1974).
Smith, Frank	*Psycholinguistics and Reading*. N.Y.: Holt, Rinehart and Winston, 1973.
Smith, Frank	*Reading without Nonsense*. N.Y.: Teacher's College Press, 1978.
Stauffer, Russell G.	*The Language Experience Approach to the Teaching of Reading*. N.Y.: Harper & Row, 1970.

Writing Research

Applebee, Arthur	*The Child's Concept of Story Ages Two to Seventeen.* Chicago: University of Chicago Press, 1978.
Bissex, Glenda	*GNYS AT WRK: A Child Learns to Write and Read.* Cambridge, MA: Harvard University Press, 1980.
Calkins, Lucy McCormick	"Children's Rewriting Strategies." *Research in the Teaching of English,* vol. 14 (Dec. 1980).
Cambourne, B., and J. Turbill	*Coping With Chaos.* Australia: Primary English Teaching Association, 1987.
Chomsky, Carol	"Write First, Read Later." *Childhood Education,* vol. 47, no. 6 (1971).
Clay, Marie	*What Did I Write?* London: Heinemann Educational Books, 1975.
De Ford, Diane E.	"Young Children and Their Writing." *Theory into Practice,* vol. 19, no. 3 (Summer 1980).
Emig, Janet	"Components of the Composing Process among Twelfth Grade Writers." Doctoral Dissertation, Harvard University, 1969.
Emig, Janet	"Non-Magical Thinking: Presenting Writing Developmentally in Schools." In *Writing: Process Development and Communication,* C. Frederickson and J. Dominic, eds., vol. 11. Hillsdale, N.J.: Erlbaum, 1981.
Graves, Donald	*Balance the Basics: Let Them Write.* N.Y.: Ford Foundation, 1978.
Graves, Donald	"The Growth and Development of First Grade Writers." Paper presented at the Canadian Council of Teachers of English Annual Meeting. Ottawa, Canada, May 1979.
Graves, Donald	*A Researcher Learns to Write.* Exeter, N.H.: Heinemann Educational Books, 1984.
Smith, Frank	*Writing and the Writer.* N.Y.: Holt, Rinehart and Winston, 1982.

Table 8.7
Whole Language Implementation Resources

Audio-Video Tapes	
Written and produced by Judith Schickeclanz	"Literacy Development in the Preschool." Portsmouth, N.H.: Heinemann Educational Books, 1987.
Donald Graves and Jane Hansen	"The Writing and Reading Process." Portsmouth, N.H.: Heinemann Educational Books, 1987.
Developed by Lucy McCormick Calkins; produced by Shelly Harwayne and Alex Mitchell	"The Writing Workshop: A World of Difference." Exeter, N.H.: Heinemann Educational Books, 1987.
Jerome Harste	"The Authoring Cycle." Portsmouth, N.H.: Heinemann Educational Books, 1985.
Carole Edelsky	"Theory and Practice in Two Meaning Centered Classrooms." N.Y.: Richard C. Owen Publishers, 1987.
Department of Education, Wellington, N.Z.	"Horrakapotchkin." N.Y.: Richard C. Owen Publishers, 1987.
Priscilla Lynch and David Doake	"Whole Language Principles and Practices in Reading Development." Toronto/ N.Y.: Scholastic, 1986.
Priscilla Lynch	"Whole Language Strategies for Upper Elementary Students." Toronto/N.Y.: Scholastic, 1986.

Table 8.8
Whole Language Teacher Resource Materials

General	
Butler, Dorothy, and Marie Clay	*Reading Begins at Home.* Portsmouth, N.H.: Heinemann, 1987.
Cochrane, Orin, Donna Cochrane, Sharen Scalena, and Ethel Buchanaan	*Reading, Writing, and Caring.* Winnepeg Whole Language Consultants. N.Y.: Richard C. Owen Publishers, 1984.
Gilles, Carol, Mary Bixby, Paul Crowley, Shirley Crenshaw, Margaret Henrichs, Frances Reynolds, and Donelle Pyle	*Whole Language Strategies for Secondary Students.* Katonah, N.Y.: Richard C. Owen Publishers, 1988.
Goodman, Kenneth S.	*What's Whole in Whole Language?* Toronto: Scholastic, 1985.
Goodman, Kenneth S., E. Brooks Smith, Robert Meredith, and Yetta Goodman	*Language and Thinking in School: A Whole Language Curriculum,* 3rd ed. Katonah, N.Y.: Richard C. Owen Publishers, 1987.
Goodman, Yetta M., Dorothy Watson, and Carolyn Burke	*Reading Miscue Inventory: Alternative Procedures.* Katonah, N.Y.: Richard C. Owen Publishers, 1987.
Hall, Nigel	*The Emergence of Literacy.* Exeter, N.H.: Heinemann Educational Books, 1987.
Heald-Taylor, B. Gail	*Whole Language Strategies for ESL Students.* Toronto: OISE, 1986.
Jaggar, Angela, and Trika Smith-Burke, eds.	*Observing the Language Learner.* Newark, Del.: International Reading Association. Co-published by the National Council of Teachers of English, 1985.
Massam, Joanna, and Anne Kulik	*And What Else?* San Diego, CA: Wright Group, 1986.
Newman, Judith	*Whole Language into Practice.* Portsmouth, N.H.: Heinemann, 1985.
Rhodes, Lynn, and C. Dudley-Marling	*Teaching and Learning Reading and Writing: Remedial and Learning Disabled Students.* Portsmouth, N.H.: Heinemann, 1988.
Steward-Dore, Nea	*Writing and Reading to Learn.* Rozelle, Australia: Primary English Teaching Association, 1986.
Strickland, Dorothy, and Joan Feeley	"Using Children's Concept of Story to Improve Reading and Writing." In T.L. Harris and E.J. Cooper, eds. *Reading, Thinking and Concept Development.* N.Y.: College Board, 1985.

Taylor, Denny	*Family Literacy*. Exeter, N.H.: Heinemann Educational Books, 1983. *Reading in Junior Classes*. Department of Education, Wellington, NZ. N.Y.: Richard C. Owen Publishers, 1985.
Watson, Dorothy, ed.	*Ideas and Insights: Language Arts K-6*. Urbana, IL: National Council of Teachers of English, 1987.

Oral Language and Drama Resources

Charters, Jill, and Anne Gately	*Drama Anytime*. Exeter, N.H.: Heinemann Educational Books, 1987.
Fox, Mem	*Teaching Drama to Young Children*. Exeter, N.H.: Heinemann Educational Books, 1987.
Judy, Susan, and Stephen Judy	*Putting on a Play*. N.Y.: Scribner, 1982.
Siks, Geraldine Brain	*Drama with Children*, 2nd ed. N.Y.: Harper & Row, 1983.

Reading Resources

Barrett, Frank	*Teacher's Guide to Shared Reading*. Toronto: Scholastic Tab Publications, 1982.
Baskwill, Jane, and Paulette Whitman	*Whole Language Sourcebook*. Toronto: Scholastic Tab Publications, 1986.
Butler, Andrea	*The Story Box in the Classroom*, Stage 1 and Stage 2. New Zealand: Shortland Publications, 1984.
Cullinan, Bernice E., Mary K. Karrer, and Arlene M. Pillar	*Literature and the Child*. N.Y.: Harcourt Brace Jovanovich, 1981.
Cullinan, Bernice E., ed.	*Children's Literature in the Reading Program*. Newark, Del: International Reading Association, 1987.
Heald-Taylor, B. Gail	*Making and Using Big Books*. Unit A 1985, Unit B 1986. Shirley Lewis Information Services, 196 North Queen Street, Toronto, Ontario, Canada, M9C 4Y1.
Hopkins, Harold R.	*From Talkers to Readers: The Natural Way*. Toronto: Ashton Scholastic, 1977.
Huck, Charlotte S., Susan Hepler, and Janet Hickman	*Children's Literature in the Elementary School*, 4th revision. N.Y.: Holt, Rinehart and Winston, 1987.
Lynch, Priscilla	*Using Big Books and Predictable Books*. Richmond Hill, Ontario: Scholastic Tab, 1986.

Mooney, Margaret	*Developing Life-Long Readers.* Wellington, NZ: Department of Education. N.Y.: Richard C. Owen Publishers, 1988.
Peetoom, Adrian	*Shared Reading: Safe Risks with Whole Books.* Richmond Hill, Ontario: Scholastic Tab, 1986.
Pulvertaft, Ann	*Carry On Reading.* Toronto: Ashton Scholastic, 1978.
Trelease, Jim	*The Read Aloud Handbook.* N.Y.: Penguin, 1982.
Van Allen, Roach, and Claryice Van Allen	*Language Experience Activities.* Boston, MA: Houghton Mifflin, 1982.
Weaver, Constance	*Reading Process and Practice.* Exeter, N.H.: Heinemann Educational Books, 1987.

Writing Resources

Atwell, Nancie	*In the Middle.* Exeter, N.H.: Heinemann Educational Books, 1987.
Calkins, Lucy McCormick	*The Art of Teaching Writing.* Portsmouth, N.H.: Heinemann Educational Books, 1986.
Calkins, Lucy McCormick, and Shelley Harwayne	*The Writing Workshop: A World of Difference.* Portsmouth, N.H.: Heinemann, 1987.
Cambourne, Brian, and Jan Turbill	*Coping with Chaos.* Australia: Primary English Teaching Association, 1987.
Clay, Marie	*What Did I Write?* London: Heinemann Educational Books, 1984.
Clay, Marie	*Writing Begins at Home.* Exeter, N.H.: Heinemann Educational Books, 1987.
Elbow, Peter	*Writing without Teachers.* N.Y.: Oxford University Press, 1973.
Frank, Marjorie	*If You're Trying to Teach Kids How to Write, You've Gotta Have This Book!.* Nashville, Tenn.: Incentive, 1979.
Fulwiler, Toby	*The Journal Book.* Exeter, N.H.: Heinemann Educational Books, 1987.
Gentry, Richard R.	*Spel . . . Is a Four Letter Word.* Richmond Hill, Ontario: Scholastic Tab, 1987.
Gordon, Naomi, ed.	*Classroom Experiences.* Exeter, N.H.: Heinemann Educational Books, 1984.
Graves, Donald, Jane Hansen, and Thomas Newkirk, eds.	*Breaking Ground.* Portsmouth, N.H.: Heinemann Educational Books, 1985.

Hansen, Jane	*When Writers Read.* Exeter, N.H.: Heinemann Educational Books, 1987.
Murray, Donald M.	*A Writer Teaches Writing.* Boston, MA: Houghton Mifflin, 1985.
Murray, Donald M.	*Write to Learn.* N.Y.: Holt, Rinehart and Winston, 1987.
Newkirk, Thomas, and Nancy Atwell	*Understanding Writing,* 2nd ed. Portsmouth, N.H.: Heinemann, 1986.
Newman, Judith	*The Craft of Children's Writing.* Toronto: Scholastic, 1984.
Smith, Frank	*Writing and the Writer.* N.Y.: Holt, Rinehart and Winston, 1982.
Temple, Charles A., Ruth G. Nathan, and Nancy Burris	*The Beginnings of Writing.* N.Y.: Allyn & Bacon, 1982.
Turbill, Jan	*No Better Way to Teach Writing.* Australia: Primary English Teaching Association, 1982.
Turbill, Jan	*Now We Want to Write.* Australia: Primary English Teaching Association, 1983.
Turbill, Jan, and Andrea Butler, eds.	*Toward a Reading-Writing Classroom.* Australia: Primary English Teaching Association, 1984.
Van Allen, Roach, and Claryce Van Allen	*Language Experience Activities.* Boston: Houghton Mifflin, 1982.
Walsh, R.D.	*Every Child Can Write.* Australia: Primary English Teaching Association, 1981.
Weiss, Harvey	*How to Make Your Own Books.* N.Y.: Crowell, 1974.

Poetry Books

Behn, Harry	*Crickets and Bullfrogs and Whispering Thunder.* Poems and Pictures by Harry Behn. Edited by Lee Bennett Hopkins. Harcourt Brace Jovanovich, 1984.
Cole, William, ed.	*An Arkful of Animals: Poems for the Very Young.* Illustrated by Lynn Munsinger. Houghton Mifflin, 1978.
Cole, William, ed.	*On Such Foolishness!* Illustrated by Tomie de Paola. Lippincott, 1978.
Cole, William, ed.	*Poem Stew.* Illustrated by Karen Weinhaus. Lippincott, 1981.
Dunning, Stephen, *et al.*, eds.	*Reflections on a Gift of Watermelon Pickle and Other Modern Verse.* Lothrop, Lee and Shepard, 1966.

Holman, Felice — *The Song in My Head.* Illustrated by Jim Spanfeller. Scribner, 1985.

Hopkins, Lee Bennett, ed. — *Moments: Poems about the Seasons.* Illustrated by Michael Hague. Harcourt Brace Jovanovich, 1980.

Hopkins, Lee Bennett, ed. — *A Song in Stone: City Poems.* Photographs by Anna Held Audette. Crowell, 1983.

Hopkins, Lee Bennett, ed. — *Pass the Poetry, Please!* Rev. ed. Harper & Row, 1987.

Kennedy, X.J. — *The Phantom Ice Cream Man: More Nonsense Verse.* Illustrated by David McPhail. Atheneum/McElderry, 1979.

Kennedy, X.J., and Dorothy M. Kennedy, authors and editors — *Knock at a Star: A Child's Introduction to Poetry.* Illustrated by Karen Ann Weinhaus. Little, Brown, 1982.

Kennedy, X.J. — *The Forgetful Wishing Well: Poems for Young People.* Illustrated by Monica Incisa. Atheneum/McElderry, 1985.

Kuskin, Karla — *Near the Window Tree: Poems and Notes.* Harper & Row, 1975.

Livingston, Myra Cohn — *Celebrations.* Illustrated by Leonard Everett Fisher. Holiday House, 1985.

Livingston, Myra Cohn, ed. — *Thanksgiving Poems.* Illustrated by Stephen Grammell. Holiday House, 1985.

Lobel, Arnold — *The Book of Pigericks.* Harper & Row, 1983.

Merriam, Eve — *Jamboree: Rhymes for All Times.* Illustrated by Walter Gaffney-Kessell. Dell, 1984.

Moore, Lillian — *Something New Begins.* Illustrated by Mary Dane Dunton. Atheneum, 1982.

O'Neill, Mary — *Hailstones and Halibut Bones.* Illustrated by Leonard Weisgard. Doubleday, 1961.

Prelutsky, Jack — *The Headless Horseman Rides Tonight.* Illustrated by Arnold Lobel. Greenwillow, 1980.

Prelutsky, Jack, ed. — *Random House Book of Poetry for Children.* Illustrated by Arnold Lobel. Random House, 1983.

Sandburg, Carl — *Early Moon.* Illustrated by James Daugherty. Harcourt Brace, 1930.

Sandburg, Carl — *Rainbows Are Made.* Compiled by Lee Bennett Hopkins. Illustrated by Fritz Eichenberg. Harcourt Brace Jovanovich, 1982.

Silverstein, Shel	*Where the Sidewalk Ends.* Harper & Row, 1974.
Silverstein, Shel	*A Light in the Attic.* Harper & Row, 1981.
Yolen, Jane, ed.	*The Lullaby Song Book.* Illustrated by Charles Mikolaycak. Harcourt Brace Jovanovich, 1986.

Classroom Materials

Reading

Colgin, Mary Lou	*Chants for Children.* Colgin, 1982.
Department of Education, Wellington, New Zealand	*Ready to Read.* (Distributed by Richard C. Owen Publishers, U.S.A., or Holt, Rinehart and Winston, Canada.)
Ginn	*Journeys in Reading through the Language Arts (K to 6).* Toronto: Ginn & Co., 1984.
Holt	*Impressions (K to 6).* Toronto: Holt, Rinehart and Winston, 1984.
Melser, June	*The Story Box.* New Zealand: Shortland Publications, 1983. (Distributed by Wright Group U.S.A., or Ginn, Canada.)
Nelson	*Networks (K to 6).* Toronto: Nelson, Canada, 1985.
Harcourt Brace Jovanovich	*Imagination, An Odyssey through Language.* Harcourt Brace Jovanovich, 1988.
Scholastic Tab	*31 Program (Grades 2 to 6).* Toronto: Scholastic Tab, 1984.
Scholastic Tab	*Whole Language Starter Kit (K to 1).* Toronto: Scholastic Tab, 1986.
Scholastic Tab	*Predictable Book Collections (Grades K to 1).* Toronto: Scholastic Tab, 1986.
Scholastic Tab	*Shared Reading Materials (K to 6) with Listening Cassette Tapes.* Toronto: Scholastic 1986.

Predictable Pattern Books for Shared-Reading

Most Predictable

Althea	*Can You Moo?* London: Dinosaur Press, 1981.
Carle, Eric	*What's for Lunch?* N.Y.: Putnam, 1982.
Duke, Kate	*Guinea Pig ABC.* N.Y.: Dutton, 1982.
Duke, Kate	*Guinea Pigs Far and Near.* N.Y.: Dutton, 1984.
Gibbons, Gail	*Trucks.* N.Y.: Crowell, 1981.

Ginsburg, Mirra	*Kittens from One to Ten.* N.Y.: Crown, 1980.
Hands, Hargrave	*Bunny Sees.* London: Walker, 1985.
Hands, Hargrave	*Duckling Sees.* London: Walker, 1985.
Hands, Hargrave	*Little Goat Sees.* London: Walker, 1985.
Hands, Hargrave	*Little Lamb Sees.* London: Walker, 1985.
Hands, Hargrave	*Puppy Sees.* London: Walker, 1985.
Hawkins, Colin, and Jacqui Hawkins	*Old Mother Hubbard.* N.Y.: Putnam, 1985.
Hill, Eric	*Where's Spot?* N.Y.: Putnam, 1980.
Langstaff, John	*Oh A-Hunting We Will Go.* N.Y.: Atheneum, 1984.
Lobel, Arnold	*On Market Street.* Toronto: Scholastic, 1981.
Parish, Peggy	*I Can, Can You?* N.Y.: Greenwillow, 1980.
Prater, John	*On Friday Something Funny Happened.* London: Puffin, 1985.
Rockwell, Anne	*Planes.* N.Y.: Dutton, 1985.
Rose, Gerald	*Trouble in the Ark.* London: Bodley Head, 1985.
Tafuri, Nancy	*Have You Seen My Duckling?* N.Y.: Greenwillow, 1984.
Watanabe, Shigeo	*Hallo, How Are You?* N.Y.: Penguin Books, 1979.
Wildsmith, Brian	*Cat on the Mat.* Toronto: Oxford, 1982.
Wildsmith, Brian	*Toot Toot.* London: Oxford, 1984.
Ziefert, Harriet	*Where Is My Dinner?* N.Y.: Putnam, 1985.
Ziefert, Harriet	*Where Is My Family?* N.Y.: Putnam, 1985.
Ziefert, Harriet	*Where Is My Friend?* N.Y.: Putnam, 1985.

Very Predictable

Bayer, Jane	*A, My Name Is Alice.* N.Y.: Dutton, 1984.
Ginsburg, Mirra	*Across the Stream.* N.Y.: Puffin, 1985.
Goss, Janet L., and Jerome Harste	*It Didn't Frighten Me.* Worthington, OH: Willowisp, 1985.
Hill, Eric	*Spot Goes to the Beach.* N.Y.: Putnam, 1985.
Hines, Anna Grossnickle	*Come to the Meadow.* Boston, MA: Houghton Mifflin, 1984.

Hooper, Meredith	*Seven Eggs.* London: Patrick Hardy, 1985.
Luton, Mildred	*Little Chick's Mothers: And All the Others.* N.Y.: Viking, 1983.
Rockwell, Anne	*Boats.* N.Y.: Dutton, 1982.
Roffey, Maureen	*Home Sweet Home.* London: Bodley Head, 1983.
Roffey, Maureen	*Look, There's My Hat.* London: Bodley Head, 1984.

Predictable Selections

Allen, Pamela	*Who Sank the Boat?* London: Hamish Hamilton, 1982.
Bauer, Caroline Feller	*My Mom Travels a Lot.* N.Y.: Warne, 1981.
Bayley, Nicola	*Spider Cat.* London: Walker, 1984.
Brett, Jan	*Annie and the Wild Animals.* Boston, MA: Houghton Mifflin, 1985.
Brown, Ruth	*If at First You Do Not See.* London: Anderson, 1985.
Brown, Ruth	*The Big Sneeze.* N.Y.: Lothrop, Lee and Shepard, 1985.
Chase, Edith Newlin and Barbara Reid	*The New Baby Calf.* Toronto: Scholastic, 1984.
Degen, Bruce	*Jamberry.* N.Y.: Harper & Row, 1983.
Duke, Kate	*Seven Froggies Went to School.* N.Y.: Dutton, 1985.
Grindley, Sally	*Knock, Knock, Who's There?* London: Hamish Hamilton, 1985.
Lobel, Arnold	*The Rose in My Garden.* N.Y.: Greenwillow, 1984.
Mayer, Mercer	*Just Grandma and Me.* Racine, Wis.: Golden Books, 1983.
Murphy, Jill	*Peace at Last.* N.Y.: Dial, 1980.
Stinson, Kathy	*Big or Little?* Toronto: Annick, 1984.
Szekeres, Cyndy	*Puppy Too Small.* Racine, Wis.: Golden Books, 1984.
Wood, Audrey	*Quick as a Cricket.* Purton, England: Child's Play (International), 1982.
Wood, Audrey	*The Napping House.* N.Y.: Harcourt Brace Jovanovich, 1984.
Zolotow, Charlotte	*Some Things Go Together.* N.Y.: Crowell, 1983.

BIBLIOGRAPHY

Aitchison, J. *Articulate Mammal*. London: Hutchinson, 1973.

Allen, Pamela. *Who Sank the Boat?* London: Hamish Hamilton Children's Books, 1982.

Allington, Richard L., and Anne McGill-Frazen. "Word Identification, Errors in Isolation and in Context: Apples vs. Oranges." *The Reading Teacher*, 33:795–800 (April 1980).

Althea. *Can You Moo?* London: Dinosaur Press, 1981.

Applebee, Arthur. *The Child's Concept of Story Ages Two to Seventeen*. Chicago: University of Chicago Press, 1978.

———. "Children's Narratives: New Directions." *The Reading Teacher*, vol. 34:137–142 (Nov. 1980).

Atwell, Nancie. *In the Middle*. Exeter, N.H.: Heinemann, 1987.

Baghban, M. J. M. *Our Daughter Learns to Read and Write: A Case Study from Birth to Three*. Newark, Del.: International Reading Association, 1984.

Baker, Evan L., and Joan L. Herman. "Educational Evaluation: Emergent Needs for Research Evaluation." *Comment*, vol. 7, no. 2:1–14 (1985).

Baskwill, Jane, and Paulette Whitman. *Whole Language Sourcebook*. Toronto: Scholastic Tab, 1986.

Barrett, Frank. *Teacher's Guide to Shared Reading*. Toronto: Scholastic Tab, 1982.

Bauer, Caroline Feller. *My Mom Travels a Lot*. N.Y.: Warne, 1981.

Bayer, Jane. *A, My Name Is Alice*. N.Y.: Dutton, 1985.

Bayley, Nicola. *Spider Cat*. London: Walker, 1984.

Behn, Harry. *Crickets and Bullfrogs and Whispering Thunder*. Poems and Pictures by Harry Behn. Edited by Lee Bennett Hopkins. Harcourt Brace Jovanovich, 1984.

Berman, P., and M. W. McLaughlin. *Federal Programs Supporting Educational Change: Factors Affecting Implementation and Continuation*, vol. 7. Santa Monica, CA: Rand, 1977.

———. *An Exploratory Study of School District Adaptation*. Santa Monica, CA: Rand, 1979.

Bettelheim, B., and K. Zelan. *On Learning to Read*. N.Y.: Knopf, 1981.

Bissex, Glenda. *GNYS AT WRK: A Child Learns to Write and Read*. Cambridge, MA: Harvard University Press, 1980.

Brett, Jan. *Annie and the Wild Animals*. Boston, MA: Houghton Mifflin, 1985.

Bridge, C.A., P. N. Winogra, and D. Haley. "Using Predictable Materials to Teach Beginning Reading." *The Reading Teacher*, 36, 884–891, 1983.

Brown, Ruth. *The Big Sneeze*. London: Stoddart, 1985.

———. *If At First You Do Not See*. London: Anderson, 1985.

Butler, Andrea. *The Story Box in the Classroom*. New Zealand: Shortland Publications, 1984.

Butler, Dorothy, and Marie Clay. *Reading Begins at Home*. Portsmouth, N.H.: Heinemann, 1987.

Calkins, Lucy McCormick. "Children's Rewriting Strategies." *Research in the Teaching of English*, vol. 14 (Dec. 1980).

———. "When Children Want to Punctuate: Basic Skills Belong in Context." *Language Arts*, 57, 567–573 (May 1980).

———. "Writing Taps a New Energy Source: The Child." *Donald Graves in Australia*. R. D. Walsh, ed. Portsmouth, N.H.: Heinemann, 45–54. 1982.

———. *Lessons from a Child*. Exeter, N.H.: Heinemann Educational Books, 1983.

———. *The Art of Teaching Writing*. Portsmouth, N.H.: Heinemann, 1986.

Calkins, Lucy McCormick, and Shelley Harwayne. *The Writing Workshop: A World of Difference*. Portsmouth, N.H.: Heinemann, 1987.

Cambourne, Brian, and Jan Turbill. *Coping with Chaos*. Australia: Primary English Teaching Association, 1987.

Campione, Joseph C., and Ann L. Brown. "Dynamic Assessment: One Approach and Some Initial Data." *Technical Report No. 361*. Urbana, Ill.: Center for the Study of Reading, 1985.

Carbo, Marie. "Reading Styles Research: What Works Isn't Always Phonics." *Phi Delta Kappan*, 68, 431–435, 1987.

Carle, Eric. *What's for Lunch?* N.Y.: Putnam, 1982.

Charters, Jill, and Anne Gately. *Drama Anytime*. Exeter, N.H.: Heinemann Educational Books, 1987.

Chase, Edith Newlin, and Barbara Reid. *The New Baby Calf*. Toronto: Scholastic, 1984.

Chomsky, Carol. *The Acquisition of Syntax from 5 to 10*. Cambridge, MA: MIT Press, 1969.

———. "Write First, Read Later." *Childhood Education*, vol. 47, no. 6 (1971).

———. "Stages in Language Development and Reading Exposure." *Harvard Educational Review*, vol. 41, no. 1 (Feb. 1972).

Clark, D. L., and E. Guba. "An Examination of Potential Change: Roles in Education." Paper presented on Innovation and Planning Social Curriculum, Oct. 1965.

Cochrane, Orin, Donna Cochrane, Sharen Scalena and Ethel Buchanan. *Reading, Writing and Caring*. Katonah, N.Y.: Richard C. Owen Publisher, 1984.

Clay, Marie M. *What Did I Write?* London: Heinemann Educational Books, 1975.

———. *Reading: The Patterning of Complex Behaviour*. London: Heinemann, 1977.

Cole, William, ed. *An Arkful of Animals: Poems for the Very Young*. Illustrated by Lynn Munsinger. Boston, MA: Houghton Mifflin, 1978.

———. *On Such Foolishness!* Illustrated by Tomie de Paola. Lippincott, 1978.

———. *Poem Stew*. Illustrated by Karen Weinhaus. Lippincott, 1981.

Colgin, Mary Lou. *Chants for Children*. Colgin, 1982.

Collins, Allan, John S. Brown, and Kathryn Larkin. "Inference in Text Understanding in Theoretical Issues." In *Reading Comprehension*, Rand J. Spiro, Bertram C. Bruce, and William C. Brewer, eds. Hillsdale, N.J.: Erlbaum, 1980.

Cox, P. "Inside-out and Outside-in: Configurations of Assistance and Their Impact on School Improvement Efforts." Paper presented at the American Educational Research Association Annual Meeting, 1983.

Cullinan, Bernice E., ed. *Children's Literature in the Reading Program.* Newark, DE: International Reading Association, 1987.

Cullinan, Bernice E., Mary K. Karrer, and Arlene Pillar. *Literature and the Child.* N.Y.: Harcourt Brace Jovanovich, 1981.

Darling-Hammond, Linda, and Arthur E. Wise. "Beyond Standardization: State Standards and School Improvement." *Elementary School Journal,* vol. 85, 316–336 (Jan. 1985).

De Ford, Diane E. "Young Children and Their Writing." *Theory into Practice,* vol. 19, no. 3 (Summer 1980).

———. "Literacy: Reading, Writing and Other Essentials." *Language Arts,* 58, 652–658 (Sept. 1981).

Degen, Bruce. *Jamberry.* N.Y.: Harper & Row, 1983.

Dewey, John. *The Child and the Curriculum.* Chicago: University of Chicago Press, 1902.

———. *Sources of a Science of Education.* N.Y.: Liveright, 1929.

———. "Experience, Nature and Art." *Art and Education.* N.Y.: Barnes, 3–12, 1929.

Doake, David. "Book Experience and Emergent Reading Behaviour." Paper presented at the Preconvention Institute, International Reading Association Annual Convention: Atlanta, GA, 2 (April 1979).

———. *Report on the Shared Book Experience Approach to Learning to Read.* Wolfville, Nova Scotia: Acadia University School of Education: 13 (April 1980).

Duke, Kate. *Guinea Pig ABC.* N.Y.: Dutton, 1982.

———. *Guinea Pigs Far and Near.* N.Y.: Dutton, 1984.

———. *Seven Froggies Went to School.* N.Y.: Dutton, 1985.

Dunning, Stephen et al., eds. *Reflections on a Gift of Watermelon Pickle and Other Modern Verse.* N.Y.: Lothrop, Lee and Shepard, 1966.

Durkin, Dolores. *Children Who Read Early.* N.Y.: Teachers College Press, 1966.

———. "Testing in Kindergarten." *The Reading Teacher,* vol. 40, no. 8:766–770 (April 1987).

Elbow, Peter. *Writing without Teachers.* N.Y.: Oxford University Press, 1973.

Elley, Warwick B., and Francis Mangubhai. "The Impact of Reading on Second Language Learning." *Reading Research Quarterly,* 19, 53–67 (Fall 1983).

Emig, Janet. "Components of the Composing Process among Twelfth Grade Writers." Doctoral Dissertation, Harvard University, 1969.

———. "Non-magical Thinking: Presenting Writing Developmentally in Schools." In *Writing: Process Development and Communication,* C. Frederickson and J. Dominic, eds., Hillsdale, N.J.: Erlbaum, 1981.

Farr, Roger, and Robert F. Carey. *Reading: What Can Be Measured?* Newark, Del.: International Reading Association, 1986.

Ferreiro, Emelia, and Anna Teberosky. *Literacy before Schooling*. Portsmouth, N.H.: Heinemann Educational Books, 1982.

Fisher, Charles W., David Berliner, Nikola Filby, Richard Marliave, Leonard Cahen, Marilyna Dishaw, and Jeffrey Moore. "Teaching and Learning in Elementary Schools: A Summary of the Beginning." *Teacher Evaluation Study*. San Francisco, CA: Far West Regional Laboratory for Educational Research and Development, 1978.

Fox, M. *Teaching Drama to Young Children*. Exeter, N.H.: Heinemann, 1987.

Frank, Marjorie. *If You're Trying to Teach Kids How to Write, You've Gotta Have This Book!* Nashville, Tenn.: Incentive, 1979.

Fullan, M. *The Meaning of Educational Change*. Toronto: OISE, 1982.

———. "Change Processes and Strategies at the Local Level." *The Elementary School Journal*, vol. 85, no. 3: 418–421, 1985.

Fulwiler, Toby. *The Journal Book*. Exeter, N.H.: Heinemann Educational Books, 1987.

Genishi, Celia, and Anne Dyson. *Language Assessment in the Early Years*. Norwood, N.J.: Ablex, 1984.

Gentry, Richard R. *Spel . . . Is a Four Letter Word*. Richmond Hill, Ontario: Scholastic Tab, 1987.

Gibbons, Gail. *Trucks*. N.Y.: Crowell, 1981.

Gilles, Carol, Mary Bixby, Paul Crowley, Shirley Crenshaw, Margaret Henrichs, Frances Reynolds, and Donelle Pyle. *Whole Language Strategies for Secondary Students*. Katonah, N.Y.: Richard C. Owen Publishers, 1988.

Ginn. *Journeys in Reading through the Language Arts*. Toronto: Ginn, Canada, 1984.

Ginsburg, Mirra. *Kittens from One to Ten*. N.Y.: Crown, 1980.

———. *Across the Stream*. N.Y.: Puffin, 1985.

Goodman, Kenneth S. "The Key Is in Children's Language." *The Reading Teacher*, vol. 25 (March 1972).

———. "Effective Teachers of Reading Know Language and Children." *Elementary English*, vol. 51, no. 6 (Sept. 1974).

———. "Acquiring Literary Is Natural: Who Skilled Cock Robin?" *Theory in Practice*, vol. 16, no. 5: 311, 1977.

———. *What's Whole in Whole Language?* Toronto: Scholastic, 1985.

———, E. Brooks Smith, Robert Meredith, and Yetta Goodman. *Language and Thinking in School: A Whole Language Curriculum*, 3rd ed. Katonah, N.Y.: Richard C. Owen Publishers, 1987.

———, Patrick Shannon, Yvonne Freeman, Sharon Murphy. *Report Card on Basal Readers*. Katonah, N.Y.: Richard C. Owen Publishers, 1988.

Goodman, Yetta. "Test Review: Concepts about Print Test." *The Reading Teacher*, vol. 34, 144–149, Jan. 1981.

———, Dorothy Watson, and Carolyn Burke. *Reading Miscue Inventory: Alternative Procedures*. Katonah, N.Y.: Richard C. Owen Publishers, 1987.

Gordon, Naomi, ed. *Classroom Experiences*. Exeter, N.H.: Heinemann Educational Books, 1984.

Graves, Donald. *Balance the Basics: Let Them Write.* N.Y.: Ford Foundation, 1978.

———. "The Growth and Development of First Grade Writers." Paper presented at the Canadian Council of Teachers of English Annual Meeting. Ottawa, May 1979.

———. *Donald Graves in Australia,* R. D. Walsh, ed. Exeter, N.H.: Heinemann, 1982.

———. *Writing: Teachers and Children at Work.* Exeter, N.H.: Heinemann, 1983.

———. *A Researcher Learns to Write.* Exeter, N.H.: Heinemann Educational Books, 1984.

———, Jane Hansen, and Thomas Newkirk, eds. *Breaking Ground.* Portsmouth, N.H.: Heinemann Educational Books, 1985.

Grindley, Sally. *Knock, Knock, Who's There?* London: Hamish Hamilton, 1985.

Hall, Nigel. *The Emergence of Literacy.* Exeter, N.H.: Heinemann Educational Books, 1987.

Halliday, Michael. *Learning How to Mean.* London: Arnold, 1975.

Hands, Hargrave. *Puppy Sees.* London: Walker, 1985.

———. *Little Lamb Sees.* London: Walker, 1985.

———. *Duckling Sees.* London: Walker, 1985.

———. *Little Goat Sees.* London: Walker, 1985.

———. *Bunny Sees.* London: Walker, 1985.

Hansen, Jane. *When Writers Read.* Exeter, N.H.: Heinemann Educational Books, 1987.

Harcourt Brace Jovanovich. *Odyssey (K to 6).* Harcourt Brace Jovanovich, 1986.

Harste, Jerome. *It Didn't Frighten Me.* Florida: School Book Fairs, 1981.

Harste, Jerome, Virginia A. Woodward, and Carolyn L. Burke. *Language Stories and Literacy Lessons.* Portsmouth, N.H.: Heinemann, 1984.

Havelock, R. G. *Planning for Innovation.* Center for Research on Utilization of Scientific Knowledge, Institute of Social Research, University of Michigan, Ann Arbor, 1971.

Hawkins, Colin, and Jacqui Hawkins. *Old Mother Hubbard.* N.Y.: Putnam, 1985.

Heald-Taylor, B. Gail. "Reading and Writing: The Natural Language Approach from Theory to Practice." Unpublished Master's Project, College of Education, Brock University, St. Catharines, Ontario, 1983.

———. "Scribble in First Grade Writing." *The Reading Teacher,* vol. 38, no. 1, Oct. 1984.

———. *Making and Using Big Books.* Unit A 1985, Unit B 1986. Toronto: Shirley Lewis Information Services, Toronto.

———. *Whole Language Strategies for ESL Students.* Toronto: OISE, 1986.

Hiebert, E. H. "Developmental Patterns and Interrelationships of Preschool Children's Print Awareness." *Reading Research Quarterly,* 16, 236–260, 1981.

Hill, Eric. *Where's Spot?* N.Y.: Putnam, 1980.

———. *Spot Goes to the Beach.* N.Y.: Putnam, 1985.

Hines, Anna Grossnickle. *Come to the Meadow.* Boston, MA: Houghton Mifflin, 1984.

Holdaway, Don. *Foundations of Literacy.* Toronto: Ashton Scholastic, 1979.
————. *Independence in Reading.* Toronto: Ashton Scholastic, 1980.
Holman, Felice. *The Song in My Head.* Illustrated by Jim Spanfeller. N.Y.: Scribner, 1985.
Holt. *Impressions.* Toronto: Holt, Rinehart and Winston, 1984.
Hooper, Meredith. *Seven Eggs.* London: Patrick Hardy, 1985.
Hopkins, Harold R. *From Talkers to Readers: The Natural Way.* Toronto: Ashton Scholastic, 1977.
Hopkins, Lee Bennett, ed. *Moments: Poems about the Seasons.* Illustrated by Michael Hague. Harcourt Brace Jovanovich, 1980.
————. *A Song in Stone: City Poems.* Photographs by Anna Held Audette. Crowell, 1983.
————. *Pass the Poetry, Please!,* rev. ed. N.Y.: Harper & Row, 1987.
Huberman, M., and D. Crandall. *People, Policies and Practices: Examining the Chain of School Improvement,* vol. 9., *Implications for Action, A Study of Dissemination Efforts Supporting School Improvement.* Andover, MA: The Network, 1983.
Huck, Charlotte S., Susan Hepler, and Janet Hickman. *Children's Literature in the Elementary School,* 4th ed. N.Y.: Holt, Rinehart and Winston, 1987.
Jaggar, Angela, and Trika Smith-Burke, eds. *Observing the Language Learner.* Newark, Del.: International Reading Association. Co-published by the National Council of Teachers of English, 1985.
Jensen, Julie M., ed. *Composing and Comprehending.* Urbana, Ill.: NCTE/ERIC, 1984.
Johnston, Peter. "Teachers as Evaluation Experts." *The Reading Teacher,* vol. 40, no. 8: 741–743, April 1987.
Joyce, B., and B. Showers. "Improving Inservice Training: The Messages from Research." *Educational Leadership,* vol. 37: 379–385, 1980.
Kennedy, X. J. *The Phantom Ice Cream Man: More Nonsense Verse.* Illustrated by David McPhail. Atheneum/McElderry, 1979.
———— and Dorothy M. Kennedy, authors and editors. *Knock at a Star: A Child's Introduction to Poetry.* Illustrated by Karen Ann Weinhaus. Boston, MA: Little, Brown, 1982.
————. *The Forgetful Wishing Well: Poems for Young People.* Illustrated by Monica Incisa. Atheneum/McElderry, 1985.
Koch, R. "Syllogisms and Superstitions: The Current State of Responding to Writing." *Language Arts,* vol. 59, no. 5, May 1982.
Kuskin, Karla. *Near the Window Tree.* N.Y.: Harper & Row, 1975.
Langstaff, John. *Oh A-Hunting We Will Go.* N.Y.: Atheneum, 1984.
Leithwood, Kenneth A. "The Principal's Role in Improving School Effectiveness: State-of-the-Art of Research in Canada." International School Improvement Project presented at the ISIP Conference, West Palm Beach, FL, Nov. 1982.
———— and Mary Stager. "Differences in Problem-Solving Processes Used by Mod-

erately and Highly Effective Principals." Paper presented at the Annual Meeting of the American Federation Research Association. San Francisco, April 1986.

Livingston, Myra Cohn. *Celebrations*. Illustrated by Leonard Everett Fisher. Holiday House, 1985.

———, ed. *Thanksgiving Poems*. Illustrated by Stephen Grammell. Holiday House, 1985.

Lobel, Arnold. *On Market Street*. Toronto: Scholastic, 1981.

———. *The Book of Pigericks*. N.Y.: Harper & Row, 1983.

———. *The Rose in My Garden*. N.Y.: Greenwillow, 1984.

Louis, Karen Seashore. "Reforming Secondary Schools: A Critique and an Agenda for Administrators." *Educational Leadership*, Sept. 1986.

Luton, Mildred. *Little Chick's Mothers: And All the Others*. N.Y.: Viking, 1983.

Lutz, J. "Some Comments on Psycholinguistic Research and Education." *The Reading Teacher*, Oct. 1974.

Lynch, Priscilla. *Using Big Books and Predictable Books*. Richmond Hill, Ontario: Scholastic Tab, 1986.

MacDonald, B., and R. Walker. *Changing the Curriculum*. London: Open Books, 1976.

Martin, N., P. D'Arcy, B. Newton, and R. Parker. *Writing and Learning across the Curriculum*. London: Ward Lock Educational, 1976.

Massam, Joanne, and Anne Kulik. *And What Else?* San Diego, CA: Wright, 1986.

Mayer, Mercer. *Just Grandma and Me*. Wis.: Golden Books, 1983.

Melser, June. *The Story Box*. New Zealand: Shortland Publications, 1983. Distributed by Wright Group, USA, or Ginn and Company, Canada.

Merriam, Eve. *Jamboree: Rhymes for All Times*. Illustrated by Walter Gaffney-Kessell. N.Y.: Dell, 1984.

Moore, Lillian. *Something New Begins*. Illustrated by Mary Dane Dunton. N.Y.: Atheneum, 1982.

Murphy, Jill. *Peace at Last*. N.Y.: Dial, 1980.

Murray, Donald M. *A Writer Teaches Writing*. Boston, MA: Houghton Mifflin, 1985.

———. *Write to Learn*. N.Y.: Holt, Rinehart and Winston, 1987.

Nelson Canada. *Networks*. Toronto: Nelson Canada, 1985.

Newkirk, Thomas, and Nancy Atwell. *Understanding Writing*, 2nd ed. Portsmouth, N.H.: Heinemann, 1986.

Newman, Judith. *Whole Language into Practice*. Portsmouth, N.H.: Heinemann, 1985.

O'Neill, Mary. *Hailstones and Halibut Bones*. Illustrated by Leonard Weisgard. N.Y.: Doubleday, 1961.

Parish, Peggy. *I Can, Can You?* N.Y.: Greenwillow, 1980.

Pearson, P. David, and Rand J. Spiro. "Toward a Theory of Leading Comprehension." *Topics in Language Disorders*, vol. 1: 71–88, Dec. 1980.

————. "Changing the Face of Reading Comprehension." *The Reading Teacher,* vol. 38: 724–738, April 1985.

————, and David B. Dunning. "The Impact of Assessment on Reading Instruction." *Illinois Reading Council Journal,* vol. 3: 18–19, Fall 1985.

Peetoom, Adrian. *Shared Reading: Safe Risks with Whole Books.* Richmond Hill, Ontario: Scholastic Tab, 1986.

Phinney, Margaret. Unpublished report, 1986.

Piaget, Jean. *The Origins of Intelligence in Children.* International Universities Press, 1952.

————. *Science of Education and the Psychology of the Child.* N.Y.: Viking, 1971.

Prater, John. *On Friday Something Funny Happened.* London: Puffin, 1985.

Prelutsky, Jack. *The Headless Horseman Rides Tonight.* Illustrated by Arnold Lobel. Greenwillow, 1980.

————, ed. *Random House Book of Poetry for Children.* Illustrated by Arnold Lobel. N.Y.: Random House, 1983.

Pulvertaft, Ann. *Carry on Reading.* Toronto: Ashton Scholastic, 1978.

Purkey, Stewart C., and Marshall S. Smith. "Effective Schools: A Review." *The Elementary School Journal,* vol. 83, no. 4: 418–452, 1983.

————. "School Reform: The District Policy Implications of the Effective Schools Literature." *The Elementary School Journal,* vol. 85: 353–390, 1985.

Read, Charles. "Children's Categorization of Speech Sounds in English." *NCTE Research Report #17.* Urbana, Ill.: NCTE, 1975.

————. "Pre-school Children's Knowledge of English Phonology." *Harvard Educational Review* 41: 1–34, 1971.

Rhodes, Lynn, and C. Dudley-Marling. *Teaching and Learning Reading and Writing: Remedial and Learning Disabled Students.* Portsmouth, N.H.: Heinemann, 1988.

Rockwell, Anne. *Boats.* N.Y.: Dutton, 1982.

————. *Planes.* N.Y.: Dutton, 1985.

Roffey, Maureen. *Home Sweet Home.* London: Bodley Head, 1983.

————. *Look, There's My Hat!* Toronto: Bodley Head, 1984.

Rogers, E. M. "Innovations in Organizations, New Research Approaches." Paper presented at the Annual Meeting of the American Political Science Association. San Francisco, Sept. 1975.

Rose, Gerald. *Trouble in the Ark.* London: Bodley Head, 1985.

Ruth, Leo. "Reading Children's Writing." *The Reading Teacher,* vol. 40, no. 8: 756–760, April 1970.

Sampson, M. R., and J. White. "The Effect of Student-authored Materials on the Performance of Beginning Readers." Paper presented at the thirty-second annual meeting of the National Reading Conference, Clearwater, FL, 1982.

Sandburg, Carl. *Early Moon.* Illustrated by James Daugherty. New York: Harcourt Brace, 1930.

————. *Rainbows Are Made.* Compiled by Lee Bennett Hopkins. Illustrated by Fritz Eichenberg. New York: Harcourt Brace Jovanovich, 1982.

Scholastic Tab. 31 Program (Grades 2–6). Toronto: Scholastic Tab, 1984.
———. Shared Reading Materials (K-6), with Listening Cassette Tapes. Toronto: Scholastic, 1986
———. Whole Language Starter Kit (K-1). Toronto: Scholastic Tab, 1986.
———. Predictable Book Collections, Grade K-1. Toronto: Scholastic Tab, 1986.
Shannon, Patrick. "Teachers' and Administrators' Thoughts on Changes in Reading Instruction within Merit Pay Program Based on Test Scores." Reading Research Quarterly, vol. 21: 20–35, Winter 1986.
Shavelson, Richard, and Paula Stern. "Research on Teachers' Pedagogical Thoughts, Judgments, Decisions and Behaviours." Review of Educational Research, vol. 41: 455–498, Winter 1981.
Showers, B. "Coaching: A Training Component for Facilitating Transfer of Training." Paper presented at the Annual Meeting of the American Educational Research Association. Montreal, 1983a.
———. "Transfer of Training." Paper presented at the Annual Meeting of the American Educational Research Association. Montreal, 1983b.
Siks, Geraldine Brain. Drama with Children, 2nd ed. N.Y.: Harper & Row, 1983.
Silverstein, Shel. Where the Sidewalk Ends. N.Y.: Harper & Row, 1974.
———. A Light in the Attic. N.Y.: Harper & Row, 1981.
Slobin, Dan. The Cross-Linguistic Study of Language Acquisition, D. Slobin, ed. Hillsdale, N.J.: Erlbaum, 1985.
Smith, Frank. Understanding Reading. Toronto: Holt, Rinehart and Winston, 1971.
———. Writing and the Writer. N.Y.: Holt, Rinehart and Winston, 1982.
———. Psycholinguistics and Reading. N.Y.: Holt, Rinehart and Winston, 1973.
———. Essays into Literacy. Exeter, N.H.: Heinemann, 1983.
Southgate, Vera, Helen Arnold and Sandra Johnson. Extending Beginning Reading. London: Heinemann Educational Books, 1981.
Spiro, Rand J., and Ann Meyers. "Individual Differences and Underlying Cognitive Processes." In Handbook of Reading Research, P. David Pearson, ed. N.Y.: Longman, 471–504, 1984.
Stallings, J. Testing Teachers' In-Class Instruction and Measuring Change Resulting from Staff Development. Mountain View, CA: Teaching and Learning Institute, 1981.
Stauffer, Russell G. The Language Experience Approach to the Teaching of Reading. N.Y.: Harper & Row, 1970.
Steward-Dore, Nea. Writing and Reading to Learn. Rozelle, Australia: Primary English Teaching Association, 1986.
Stinson, Kathy. Big or Little? Toronto: Annick, 1984.
Strickland, Dorothy, and Joan Feeley. "Using Children's Concept of Story to Improve Reading and Writing." In T. L. Harris and E. J. Cooper, eds. Reading, Thinking and Concept Development. N.Y.: College Board, 1985.
Sulzby, Elizabeth. "Children's Emergent Abilities to Read Favorite Storybooks." Final Report to the Spencer Foundation. Evanston, Ill.: Northwestern University, 1983.

———. "Children's Emergent Reading of Favourite Storybooks: A Developmental Study." *Reading Research Quarterly,* vol. 20: 458–481, Summer 1985.

———, and William Teale. "Writing Development in Early Childhood." *Educational Horizons,* vol. 64: 8–12, Fall 1985.

———. *Emergent Literacy: Writing and Reading.* Norwood, N.J.: Ablex, 1987.

Szekeres, Cyndy. *Puppy Too Small.* Racine, WI: Golden Book, 1984.

Tafuri, Nancy. *Have You Seen My Duckling?* N.Y.: Greenwillow, 1984.

Taylor, Denny. *Family Literacy.* Exeter, N.H.: Heinemann Educational Books, 1983.

Teale, William H., Elfrieda H. Hiebert, and Edward A. Chittenden. "Assessing Young Children's Literary Development." *The Reading Teacher,* vol. 40, no. 8: 772–777, April 1987.

Temple, Charles A., Ruth G. Nathan, and Nancy Burris. *The Beginning of Writing.* N.Y.: Allyn & Bacon, 1982.

Thorn, Elizabeth. *Teaching the Language Arts.* Toronto: Gage Educational Publishing, 1974.

Trelease, Jim. *The Read Aloud Handbook.* N.Y.: Penguin Books, 1982.

Turbill, Jan. *Now We Want to Write.* Australia: Primary English Teaching Association, 1983.

———, and Andrea Butler, eds. *Toward a Reading-Writing Classroom.* Australia: Primary English Teaching Association, 1984.

Valencia, Sheila, and David Pearson. "Reading Assessment: Time for a Change." *The Reading Teacher,* vol. 40, no. 8: 726, April 1987.

Van Allen, Roach, and Claryce Van Allen. *Language Experience Activities.* Boston, MA: Houghton Mifflin, 1982.

Watanabe, Shigeo. *Hallo, How Are You?* N.Y.: Penguin Books, 1979.

Watson, Dorothy, ed. *Ideas and Insights: Language Arts K-6.* Urbana, Ill.: National Council of Teachers of English, 1987.

Weaver, Constance. *Reading Process and Practice.* Exeter, N.H.: Heinemann Educational Books, 1987.

———. *Reading Process and Practice.* Portsmouth, N.H.: Heinemann, 1988.

Weiss, Harvey. *How to Make Your Own Books.* N.Y.: Crowell, 1974.

Wells, Gordon. *Language Development in the Pre-school Years.* Cambridge: Cambridge University Press, 1985.

———. *The Meaning Makers: Children Learning Language and Using Language to Learn.* Portsmouth, N.H.: Heinemann Educational Books, 1986.

Wildsmith, Brian. *Cat on the Mat.* Toronto: Oxford, 1982.

———. *Toot Toot.* London: Oxford, 1984.

Wilson, R. G. "The Effects of District-wide Variables on Student Achievement." In K. A. Leithwood and A. Hughes, eds. *Curriculum Canada III.* Vancouver: University of British Columbia: 73–88, 1981.

Wittrock, Merlin C. "Process Oriented Measures of Comprehension." *The Reading Teacher,* vol. 40, no. 8: 734–737, April 1987.

Wood, Audrey. *The Napping House.* N.Y.: Harcourt Brace Jovanovich, 1984.

Wood, David, L. MacMahon, and Y. Cranstoun. *Working with Under Fives.* London: Grant McIntyre, 1980.

Yolan, Jane, ed. *The Lullaby Song Book.* Illustrated by Charles Mikolaycak. Harcourt Brace Jovanovich, 1986.

Ziefert, Harriet. *Where Is My Friend?* N.Y.: Putnam, 1985.

———. *Where Is My Family?* N.Y.: Putnam, 1985.

———. *Where Is My Dinner?* N.Y.: Putnam, 1985.

Zolotow, Charlotte. *Some Things Go Together.* N.Y.: Crowell, 1983.

Index

Art Activities. *See* Reading
Assessment. *See* Evaluation, Implementation, Reading
Drama
  pantomime, 22
  puppet plays, 23
  readers' theater, 26–27
  story-telling, 26
  See also Speaking
Evaluation
  anecdotal records, 113–114
  assessing a whole language school, 60–63
  assessing a principal's effectiveness, 78, 81
  basal assessment inventory, 89–92
  behavior inventories in listening, speaking, reading, writing, 128–143
  data collection formats, 113–115
  implementation, 51–81
  listening inventory, 114
  log books, 113, 115
  philosophy of whole language, 109–113
  principal effectiveness (*see* assessing a principal's effectiveness)
  reading, 124
  report cards for whole language, 126
  research, 124–125
  running records, 117–118
  scribble, 47, 49
  self, 118
  spelling, 117
  standardized tests, 110–112
  student, 109–143
  whole language school inventory, 62–66

  work samples, 118
  writing log, 114–116
Implementation
  areas of change, 60
  assessing principal's effectiveness in implementing whole language, 54–55, 78, 81
  assessing a whole language school, 62–66
  change (*see* areas of change)
  change process for teachers, 83–88
  continuation of change process, 76–78
  goal setting, 66–70
  implementation plan, 74–76
  initiation for change, 57–60
  plan (*see* implementation plan)
  planning for change, 57
  principal's checklist for successful, 54–55, 81
  principal's role in, 51–53, 54–55
  process of, 51–81
  progress indicators in process, 70–73
  research in, 51–53
  review for continuation (*see* continuation of change process)
  review for initiation (*see* initiation for change)
  whole language implementation process, 51–81
Parents and whole language
  birthday books for children, 106
  classroom in-service for parents, 99
  communicating with parents, 93–98
  communication strategies between school and home, 94–108

Parents and whole language (*continued*)
curriculum night for parents, 101
diary for children, 106
dictated stories, strategy for parents,
105, 106, 108
excursions for children, 108
family history, 107
gift book, 106
history (*see* family history)
informing parents about whole language,
93–94
in-service for parents, 99
letters to parents, 94–98, 101–105
literacy stories for parents, 95–98
media presentations for parents, 100
messages between parents and children,
107
newsletters for parents, 94–98
parent nights, 99
photo albums of family, 105–106
question-answer sessions for parents,
37–50
reading to children, 107–108
resources for parents, 149–174
scrapbooks, 106
story-telling, 108
student work samples, 98
tips for parents using whole language,
105–108
trip book, 106
whole language strategies for parents
(*see* tips for parents)
work samples (*see* student work samples)
written conversation for parents and
children, 107
Reading
approaches to reading (whole language
vs skills based), 7–17
art activities in reading, 29
assessing whole language school, 62–66
author studies, 28
basal reader checklist, 89–92
big books, 24
book talks, 27
buddies (reading buddies), 29
dialogue journals, 27–28
dictated sentences, 26
dictated stories, 24–25

evaluation of, 10
individualized, 27
integration with listening, speaking,
writing, 29
interpretive activities for, 28–29
literature in reading instruction, 27–28
materials for programs, 167–168, 169–
173
novel studies, 28
pattern writing, 24
peer dictation, 26
philosophy of, 8–10
phonics, 9, 10, 12–15
progress indicators in, 70–73
questions about learning, 41–47
readers' theater, 26–27
reading buddies, 29
research in, 149–151, 154–157, 163
resource materials for, 166–173
running records, 117–118
shared, 23
skills-based approach to, 6–15
story-telling, 26
themes, 22
vocabulary development, 42
whole language approach (*see* approaches to reading)
whole language behavior inventory, 127–
143
word banks, 43
Speaking
acquisition, 4–7
activities, 29. *See also* Drama
big books, 24
book talks, 27
dictated sentences, 26
dictated stories, 24–25
drama, 22–27
evaluating, 10
idea webbing, 34–35
peer dictation, 26
philosophy in, 4–7
progress indicators, 70–73
puppet plays, 23
readers' theater, 26–27
research in oral language, 152–153, 162
resource materials in oral language,
166–167
role play, 22–23

shared reading, 23
story-telling, 26
strategies in oral language, 24. *See also*
    Drama
word webbing, 34–35
Tests. *See* Evaluation
Whole Language
    approach to, 3–17
    evaluation in, 109–143
    implementation processes for, 51–81
    materials for, 166–173
    philosophy of, 4–7, 38–41
    principles of, 15–17
    professional materials for research, 149–
        185
    questions about, 37–50
    resources in, 149–185
    strategies in, 19–35, 61
    themes in, 22
Writing
    activities in, 29–34
    approaches to, 10–12, 14–15
    conferencing, 30
    conversation, written, 32–33
    dialogue journals, 27–28
    dictated sentences, 26

dictated stories, 24–25
editing, 31
evaluation of, 12, 13
folders, 31–32
handwriting, 48
idea generation, 30
idea webbing, 34, 35
integration of, with listening, speaking,
    reading, 29
journals (*see* notebook)
learning to, 34
log, 114, 116
notebook, 34
pattern, 24
peer dictation, 26
process in, 29–31
progress indicators, 70–73
publishing, 31
questions about, 47–50
research in, 158–161, 164
resources in, 165–169
revising, 30–31
scribble in the process, 47, 49
skills-based approach to, 7–15
whole language approach to, 10–13
word banks, 43
word webbing, 34–35

About the Author

Whole language education has occupied Gail Heald-Taylor for more than a decade. As vice-principal, curriculum consultant, gifted resource teacher, and classroom teacher, she has used whole language in the classroom with students, in the school to orchestrate change, and in school districts to encourage the implementation of whole language.

The author of *Whole Language and ESL, Making and Using Big Books,* and a number of journal articles, Professor Heald-Taylor teaches in the Faculty of Education, University of Windsor, Canada.